CALLED TO
BREAKTHROUGH

AN AUTOBIOGRAPHY

CALLED TO
BREAKTHROUGH

AN AUTOBIOGRAPHY

RABBI KIRT A. SCHNEIDER

CHARISMA
HOUSE

Most Charisma Media products are available at special quantity discounts for bulk purchase for sales promotions, premiums, fundraising, and educational needs. For details, call us at (407) 333-0600 or visit our website at www.charismamedia.com.

CALLED TO BREAKTHROUGH by Rabbi Kirt A. Schneider
Published by Charisma House, an imprint of Charisma Media
600 Rinehart Road, Lake Mary, Florida 32746

Visit the author's website at https://discoveringthejewishjesus.com.

Cataloging-in-Publication Data is on file with the Library of Congress.
International Standard Book Number: 978-1-62999-998-2
E-book ISBN: 978-1-62999-999-9

The author has made every effort to provide accurate accounts of events, but he acknowledges that others may have different recollections of these events. Every effort also has been made to provide accurate internet addresses at the time of publication.

21 22 23 24 25 — 987654321

Printed in the United States of America

As always, "For from Him and through Him and to Him are all things. To Him be the glory forever. Amen" (Romans 11:36).

I want to dedicate this book to my family—to Cynthia, my bride; and my two daughters, Alyssa Beth and Summer Briana, and their families.
I also want to acknowledge Michael Hardy and Dustin Roberts, who oversee and manage so much for me at Discovering the Jewish Jesus, as well as the entire DJJ staff.
Finally, although I am not able to physically get to Lion of Judah World Outreach Center as often anymore, I would like to express my love to my sons, daughters, and friends there.

CONTENTS

God has broken through my enemies by my hand, like
the breakthrough of waters.
—1 CHRONICLES 14:11

1

A HAPPY CHILDHOOD

WHEN YOU THINK of Jewish communities in the United States, I think the first place your mind goes to is New York City, not the Midwest—and definitely not Beachwood, Ohio, the suburb of Cleveland where I lived as a young boy.

But the truth is, outside of communities in Israel and New York, Beachwood has the highest concentration of Jews of anywhere in the world. The community was—and still is—roughly 90 percent Jewish. That may just sound like an interesting statistic, but for me growing up, it defined my world. I am an American by birth and nationality, but everything in the culture I grew up in was run through the lens of being Jewish.

My dad's parents immigrated to the United States in 1913 from Poland, seeking to escape growing anti-Semitism and find a better life in America. My grandfather's name was Moses Schneiderman, which morphed into Morris Schneider sometime after they got to the United States (probably to make them sound less Jewish). He and my grandmother spoke mostly Yiddish all their lives. I don't know that they ever learned more than a functional amount of English. My dad's mother stood above six feet, and my grandpa was about five feet tall. I remember her as domineering, and my dad described his father as sweet.

My grandparents both worked very hard to make it in the new country, and my dad spent a lot of time alone growing up. They had the classic immigrant story, facing numerous hardships and struggles, working their way up doing whatever jobs they could find or create, and hoping their children would live a better life than *they* had. In fact, my dad had to work after school to contribute to the family income so the family could get by, which meant he never had the opportunity to participate in after-school sports or other activities. It's amazing how eventually so many of the Jewish children whose parents came over like my dad's found niche businesses and became very successful entrepreneurs. It was as if it were in their blood.

For my dad it was selling clothing, or what they jokingly call *schmatte* ("rags") in Yiddish. He started by selling shirts, pants, and dresses out of his car, driving from one neighborhood to the next. As he scraped together enough to invest, he found a building and eventually opened Schneider's Department Store in Middlefield, Ohio, a rural community east of Cleveland that he felt was the perfect spot. It consisted of a strong Amish community and the "Yankees" (the non-Amish) who also lived in town. So in addition to selling clothing, my dad set up a fabric shop, since the Amish made their own clothing. The parking lot had spaces for the cars of the townspeople as well as for the horses and buggies the Amish would arrive in. The business grew quickly, and my parents prospered. They expanded the store to sell all types of men's, women's, and children's clothing as well as other items and accessories. They eventually opened another store in town called The She Shack, which my mom ran for a while and which sold trendy women's fashions.

We lived in Middlefield for the first year of my life before we upgraded to Beachwood about the time my brother, Mitchell, was born. The communities were close, about thirty miles apart, but being an eastern suburb of Cleveland, Beachwood had a lot more going on. With my dad's success as a businessman came many benefits and pleasures, including great food, a nice house, stylish clothes, toys, and vacations in Florida many winters. My brother and I even had minibikes. This was our lifestyle until competition started cutting into my dad's business soon after I graduated from high school.

As toddlers we had an Amish nanny and then later a live-in Amish housekeeper when we moved to Pepper Pike, where I started middle school. I'm sure Dad made the connections with our Amish nanny and housekeeper through his customers. The Amish went to school only through eighth grade, and then they were required to contribute to their community by working. Our housekeeper would come home with dad on Monday nights and return to Middlefield on Fridays. That went on for most of my teenage years.

My mom and dad were the "cool parents," and all my friends liked them. My dad had black hair that was slicked back, wore a stylish leather coat, and joked with my friends a lot. The Jewish community that I was a part of was very sociable, colorful, and expressive. When you see movies about the sixties where all the people are very trendy, barbecuing in each other's backyards, dressed in the latest fashions, drinking and laughing at each other's jokes, and, unfortunately, eyeing each other's wives, that's a lot like the place where I grew up.

My mother was very beautiful, and I remember she had a standing appointment at the beauty salon every Saturday. She was always dressed to impress, even when just staying home. She was also a very self-confident woman, and I felt very close to her. She never told us much about her family's background.

She was always supportive of me, and I think a lot of my early confidence in life came from that support and how confidently she carried herself. She was always available to Mitchell, Susie (my sister, who is four years younger), and me. Anytime we wanted to go somewhere, even when other parents weren't around or willing, I knew I could call my mom and she'd take us, whether it was to go fishing, swimming, to the mall, or to a movie. She was just always there for me. My siblings may remember it differently, but that's what I recall.

While we lived in Beachwood, my family belonged to a country club, and we would laze around the pool almost every day in the summers. When the weather was nice, we would oftentimes eat outside in the evenings. Sometimes my dad would grill something, and we would have watermelon for dessert. I remember those times very positively and warmly.

Some of my earliest memories have to do with being out in nature. Now, of course, Beachwood was a suburb, so it wasn't like I was Huck Finn on the Mississippi, but I felt like it. Beachwood was a developing community in those years, and there were still vacant lots with tall trees I could get lost among, as if they were mighty forests. We had a small backyard, but it was big enough for me. When you're a kid, even a few square feet of mud can seem like a world unto itself.

I remember lying on my back, looking up at the blue sky, and eating the wild mint that grew in our backyard in the summertime. Our yard also teemed with wildlife—grasshoppers, crickets, caterpillars, fireflies, and the like. I would catch anything I could put in a jar, then sit and watch it. When we went on vacation to Miami Beach during winter break, I would catch these green lizards that could turn brown to camouflage themselves. I snuck them on the plane to take them home and tried to feed, nurture, and take care of them. I got totally immersed in looking at the lizards and the other creatures I'd caught.

One time I caught a fish with my hands in a friend's pond and brought it home in a bucket. We had a kiddie pool we put in the backyard in the summer, so I took that into the basement, filled it with water, and put the fish in it. I remember watching it swim all around. It was mesmerizing. A friend and I also raised mice in his basement, but I lost interest in the mice after I got bitten.

The country club we belonged to was near a wooded creek. While my mom would lie out in the sun and Mitchell and Susie would swim and play, I used to go out exploring, catching frogs and snakes there. The smells, colors, and beauty engulfed me.

We had this little blue plastic boat that was designed to be a swimming pool for toddlers. One time a couple of friends and I put it in the creek at the country club. While we floated along, I saw a snapping turtle surface near us, and I leaned over and grabbed it by its shell. It sparkled iridescent in the sunlight. It was such a fascinating animal! I brought it home and put it in a small aquarium. It got so big I eventually gave it to a friend who had a really big aquarium. I visited him years later, after we'd moved to Pepper Pike, and he still had it.

Looking back, there was a simple, profound sense of God I experienced as a kid. I was in my own world.

Nature was the first place where I consistently got an awareness of God's presence. Mind you, it was just a taste, and I'm sure I couldn't have told you it was God back then. But I believe it is something that stayed with me over the years and fed the yearning for knowing and feeling God that would grow as I got older. Even back then I think I knew there was something more to the world and living than just what I saw and touched. I believe God was reaching out to me at that very young age, even though He was not discussed much in the secular Jewish culture around me.

At this same time, I was becoming pretty crazy about girls, even at elementary school age. I was also just discovering the intoxicating power of music and had my first record player in my room. There was a song that I liked to listen to called "Michelle." I would play that song and change the name to Rochelle, because I was "in love" with a girl around the corner named Rochelle. Nothing I did at school seemed to get her attention, though, so I resorted to guerrilla tactics. I got a rubber band and a bunch of paper clips, bent the paper clips into a U shape, and then used them to shoot the backs of her bare calves. (She usually wore knee-length dresses.) As far as I knew, that still didn't get her attention, at least until her mom called my mom. With a logic that only moms can devise, my mom took me to Rochelle's house and Rochelle's mom took us to McDonald's. I guess somehow that humanized Rochelle for me, and I left her alone after that.

Then there was Cheryl, my third-grade love, who also happened to be my next-door neighbor and a couple of years older (and probably a foot taller). I fell hard for a few days. We never actually spoke, but when the neighborhood kids ran around playing together, I had a hard time taking my eyes off her. Back in those days, ID bracelets (bracelets with names on them) were popular. I remember working up the courage to ask Cheryl to "go steady" with me and wear my bracelet. (Looking back, the term we used, *going steady*, was humorously ridiculous because we never actually *went* anywhere!) When she said yes, I saw the stars! It was intoxicating—or at least it was for the next hour. It took about that long for her parents to discover the bracelet and tell her I was too young for her. Her big brother came over to our house and gave me my bracelet back, explaining that her father wouldn't let her go steady with me. But boy, was I in love *for the afternoon*! And I would continue falling "in love" with various girls while I was growing up.

My relationship with my siblings was multidimensional growing up. In some ways we got along, and in some ways we didn't. I think the sense of looking good in the eyes of the community, which my parents valued, somehow translated into a sense of competitiveness that was absorbed by us kids. I remember that Mitchell and I fought a lot as teenagers—or more truthfully I should say I picked on him a lot, something I am sorry for today. (In retrospect I strongly believe my picking on him had demonic origins.) Being so close in age was both a blessing and a curse. It meant we often did things together but also that there was a lot of fighting. I love my brother very much, and once I came to Jesus, I felt very bad about how I'd treated him growing up and tried very hard to heal it.

Susie, on the other hand, was much younger, so it wasn't the same. At times, I felt very close to my sister, particularly while I was in high school. I wanted to protect my little sister. I also felt she was inspired by me and looked up to me as her eldest brother. Unfortunately the competitive spirit in my family ended up taking deep root in my sister as well. This surfaced particularly in the area of our differing faiths later in life. She is now a rabbi in the Jewish Renewal movement (a recent movement that endeavors to reinvigorate modern Judaism), and our paths have gone in very different directions.

In terms of my relationships with my peers, I was popular and had a lot of friends all through my school years. I never tried to be popular; I just was. My parents were well-liked by all my friends, and everyone enjoyed coming over to our house. I was known as fun, daring, and a prankster. If someone was going to do something crazy just to see what would happen, it was going to be me. I'm a forerunner. I push the envelope. The Lord has used many of those attributes He placed within me to build His kingdom—but as a kid it led to some mayhem!

An example of this is when my mom took me to the pet store in the mall one time and agreed to buy me a garter snake. Afterward we went to a delicatessen that was connected to the mall. As we ate, I couldn't stop thinking about my snake, so I kept lifting the lid of its box to peek at it. That, of course, led to my wanting to take it out and play with it, and the next thing my mom knew, I'd put it on the floor. It glided across the linoleum into the midst of the other tables. It was hilarious and tragic at the same time. I don't remember my mom getting mad at me about it. She probably just said something like, "Oh, *Kirtmo*," trying not to let me see her smiling.

As you can tell by this story, my parents had a somewhat lax sense of discipline. That meant we had a lot of freedom as kids and later as teens. Although I enjoyed this freedom and have great appreciation for my parents, in time I would see that there were pitfalls in their parenting style, as I will explain in later chapters.

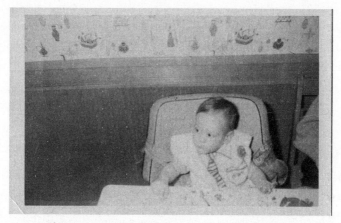

This is me at my first birthday party. Overall, I felt happy
growing up, and our house had much laughter.

It was not just my immediate family, however, that was so instrumental in my formative years; it was also the Jewish culture of our community.

2

GROWING UP JEWISH

I OFTEN FIND IT difficult to explain to non-Jews just what it was like being raised in a little Jewish bubble in the sixties and seventies. It was very typically Midwest American in many ways and not so typical in many other ways. The biggest difference was probably our sense of being separate from everyone who wasn't Jewish and closer to and "safe" with anyone who was. It's hard to describe the immediate degree of trust you have when you meet a new person who is Jewish versus meeting someone who is not. I actually have what I jokingly call "Jewdar" (like radar). Oftentimes I can discern whether someone is Jewish the instant I meet the person. It's an immediate ability to identify with and feel connected to that person despite knowing little about him or her.

I believe it comes from something that is not so much spoken as imparted. No one taught it to me; it was simply absorbed from the older generations. It's a subtle sense of trust for one another and distrust of others. I think my father had it, knowing his family had to flee its homeland due to growing anti-Semitic persecution. Jews have a deep sense in their souls that we are a people different from any other on earth but oftentimes despised and targeted for persecution.

The disturbing thing about it is that many Jews' sense of Jewishness is more cultural than spiritual. It is often totally separate from knowing or trusting in the God who chose us. My dad would say, "I'm a Jew from the top of my head to the bottom of my feet," but later in life I also remember him saying, "I don't even know if I believe in God." In the area where I grew up, we had a shared culture, shared Scriptures, shared rituals, shared community, and shared history, but our spirituality, for the most part, was a totally individual thing. Little I learned growing up as a Jew pointed me toward a personal relationship with God or gave life eternal meaning.

The Jewish people can be clannish. What I mean is that when you live with a history of persecution and you feel as if the only ones you can rely on are your own people, you become very insular. This is how Jewish people have thought and survived from the time they were slaves in Egypt. In general they live separated from everybody outside their ethnicity. Due to our history many in the older generation see the world as against them, and the only people they feel won't try to take advantage of them are other Jews.

Another thing to understand about Jewish identity is that it carries a sense of distinction through birthright. When you look at their achievements in business, medicine, industry, and theater and film, the amount of success Jewish people have had in the earth is disproportionate to their numbers. Jewish people know there is something unique about them. For some Jews, being Jewish can also include a paranoia that at the drop of a hat, as happened in Germany (and still happens from time to time today), the surrounding culture can turn on them, smash the windows of their shops, and set fire to their synagogues. It has caused the building of walls, even if they are invisible ones, between Jews and the rest of the world.

As I said, it was nothing I noticed as a child, but living in a community where being Jewish was woven into the fabric of everything—from whom we were friends with to our school holidays to how we related to one other—infused us with Jewishness from the day we were born. Being Jewish in a mostly Jewish community created feelings of camaraderie and safety. There was a sense of commonality that made growing up in a Jewish family and neighborhood really rich and good. Overall it was a colorful experience for me, with many fond memories of love, freedom, and belonging.

There is Judaism the religion and Judaism the culture. Religiously there are three general branches of Judaism—Reform, Conservative, and Orthodox—and each dictates an authentic expression of Judaism to its adherents, even though they look very different. There's Reform Judaism, which is the most modern and liberal. Reform Jews are very Jewish in terms of identity, but that identity is more based on being a part of the Jewish community than having a personal relationship with God based on the laws of the Torah. There is a deep sense of being called to do good but little sense of living by the literal Scriptures. Reform Jews have a respect for the Tanakh (an acronym for the three divisions of the Hebrew Bible: the Torah—the five books of Moses and the law, the Nevi'im—the prophets, and the Ketuvim—the writings and poetry), but it is viewed more as metaphor than anything that should be literally obeyed.

I say this very generally because there are many forms of Reform Judaism in a similar way to there being many variations of liberal Protestantism. There are some Reform Jews who would say that God is important to them, but most will give you a puzzled look if you talk about having a personal relationship with Him. Most Reform Jews are politically liberal, more looking for solutions through politics and social justice than trusting in God and following His commandments. Their view is that God is the God of creation, who set the world and universe in motion, but the rest is in our hands.

On the opposite side of the spectrum Orthodox Jews believe in God's Word as the ultimate authority for how to live and please God. If you didn't know any better, you might confuse the way they dress and how they separate themselves from society in general with the Amish, though the two groups are very, very different. In a nutshell Orthodox Jews do their best to live in alignment with the Jewish Scriptures and strive to keep themselves pure of the corrupting influences of other cultures and value systems by living separate and unto themselves.

Then you have the Conservative branch of Judaism, which was the type of synagogue that I was bar mitzvahed in. Conservative Judaism holds to the authority of God's Word—the Tanakh and the Mitzvot (the commandments given by God to be performed as a religious duty)—but they feel it's important to interpret them in a way that suits human needs today. It's kind of a middle-of-the-road approach between Reform and Orthodox Judaism. Although my family attended synagogue on holy days like Rosh Hashanah and Yom Kippur and celebrated Passover in our home, religion had very little to do with our day-to-day life. We were very secular, as was true of the Jewish friends and neighbors my parents socialized with. Being secular, we took advantage of the modern tools and methods society had to offer.

This was evident in the way they handled a problem I was having with wetting the bed at night in my sleep when I was about five or six years old. To help me, they got a machine that attached to a rubber mat and had metal wires running through it. You placed this mat on top of the mattress and under the sheets. Whenever urine went through the sheet onto the mat, the moisture would act as a conduit between the little wires, creating an electrical circuit that sounded an alarm and set off rotating lights. It had this large control box that sat in the corner of my room.

I was so embarrassed by it and did not want anyone to know what it was. When we had a babysitter, I would tell her it was a radio and not to touch it. Thankfully it did help cure me of bed wetting very quickly, and we didn't have it around for long. I don't think there was an emotional cause for my bed-wetting. Rather, it was just a developmental issue that I outgrew, as is true of most children who wet their beds.

There were other problems my parents helped me to solve as well. One I remember was when I was in fourth grade. I was having a problem with a kid in the neighborhood who threw rocks at me. The kid's house was up on a bit of a hill, and he'd throw rocks down as people went by. I remember it getting so bad I grew afraid to go by his house. When I told my dad about it, rather than calling the kid's parents, he just said, "Well, you're going to have to face the kid someday."

I got the message, and the very next day I went over to the boy's house, walked up to him, and punched him in the face. He never threw rocks at me again. I learned from my dad that day that it's best to deal with a problem head-on rather than letting it grow, even if solving it by punching someone wasn't the best of ideas.

Overall, I remember my childhood as happy and secure. I remember there being a lot of laughter—my mom and dad could be really funny—and we did a lot of fun things together. One of my best memories is when my dad bought me and my brother Western leather coats with fringes down the arms and in front. He let us pick out what color we wanted. Usually you saw people wearing these cowboy coats in brown or tan, but I chose white. I looked like a little Jewish Elvis Presley.

All through our time in Beachwood I knew my parents loved me and liked to have my siblings and me around. My dad would take us fishing and for walks in the woods, and I had a deep love for and special connection with my mom. We had freedom to roam, partly because of the times and the close-knit community and partly because we were allowed to run a little wild.

While in some ways this freedom was good—in that it gave me the confidence that I could do anything—it also proved an unstable foundation for any solid sense of identity as I grew older. The lack of boundaries left me feeling insecure and alone. I had no grid or master framework to use to interpret the world, over- come its dangers, or find any real meaning. Being raised with few real limitations was great for a while, but eventually it left me feeling lost, directionless, and unprepared for adulthood. I wouldn't be who I am today without having been raised the way I was raised. All of us are broken, so I want to bless my parents for being my parents—through the good, the bad, and the ugly.

But they were far from perfect, as is true of all of us. Something every boy needs is a father to train him, to prepare him for adult- hood, and to teach him how to be a man. Unfortunately, because my dad spent a lot of time alone growing up and wasn't very close to his own father, there were things he could not give me. On the other hand, I am who I am in the positive sense partly because of what I did receive from my father. Still, there has been a lot of pain and a lot of overcoming that I've had to do.

I don't remember when it started, but I had some pretty weird fears growing up. I was afraid of being kidnapped by monsters—the ones in my closet, the ones under the bed, and especially the one that was going to swing in through my window from the empty lot next door. I had this deep-seated image of him scooping me up and taking me back out through the window and off to who knows where. When one of those fears got really bad, I'd sneak into my brother's room and climb in bed beside him. I don't know if I thought being next to him would protect me or if it was just because his window didn't overlook an empty lot, but sometimes it was the only place I felt safe enough to go to sleep.

Another example of one of the bizarre fears that plagued me was when my family went for a cruise on a big boat. As I looked over the edge at the water, I got a panicky feeling that I would lose control and throw myself overboard. It was irrational, but I had to fight to not let it get the best of me. It was like I was afraid some outside force was going to take over my mind and make me do something against my will.

This same phenomenon plagued me as a teenager after I started driving. I feared that same force would take me over as I drove and I'd swerve into the guardrail along the side of the road or into the oncoming traffic. These random thoughts made me afraid that I would do something that I didn't want to do—that I would lose control and act out in a way that would harm me.

I also remember from time to time getting gripped with strange paranoia that would stay with me for a few months. One time in grade school I developed this obsessive-compulsive fear that if I touched something with the index finger of one hand, I had to touch it with the same finger of the other hand too, or else I would die. On a family vacation to Cape Cod I was in the backseat with Mitchell and Susie and the obsession got really bad. Fortunately it vanished as quickly as it came. It just disappeared one day, and I forgot about it, but it was tormenting while it lasted, which is why I still remember it.

Another manifestation of fear surfaced when I was in third grade. I was never the best of students. Our teachers always broke us into three reading groups according to how well we read, and I was always in the slowest. My handwriting was also very sloppy. (In fact, to this day it still is.) But I had one great moment at Hilltop Elementary School when I was eight years old. It was Safety Week. Our teachers were all teaching about things we needed to do to be safe, and there was a poster contest among the students stressing safety themes. The most outstanding posters would win prizes.

At the time, my phobia was being poisoned. For some reason I had this odd paranoia that I was going to accidentally ingest poison and then die. So I drew a picture of a medicine cabinet and a thermometer. Thermometers in those days were made of thin glass tubes with mercury inside them. (If you're of a certain age, you probably remember those!) The boy in my picture had opened the medicine cabinet, and when he did, a thermometer that was in the cabinet fell to the ground and broke. In the sketch a drop of mercury from the now-broken thermometer bounced up off the floor and went into the boy's mouth. (Mercury is poisonous!) I can't remember exactly what the boy in my drawing looked like, but I know, based on my art talent, his portrait had to be quite juvenile. The caption under my childish picture was "Beware of Poison."

Even though my cartoonish sketch was terrible (my drawing is no better than my handwriting), I won a transistor radio for placing in the top ten young artists in the school because I was the only kid who made a poster about being poisoned. Hilltop Elementary School had to cover the poison base, and I was the only one to do it. I guess in this case my paranoia paid off in a small way. I remember hearing my name called as the winner, giggling, standing up, and going forward to get my radio. I can still recall how the electronic device smelled when I took it out of its box. I'll probably never forget that.

I don't know for sure why I seemed to struggle so much with fear. I do believe that despite my confident and assertive exterior, I have a very tender and sensitive spirit. I also believe the Lord allowed me to be attacked by demonic fears of all kinds in order to prepare me to come to Him and become an overcomer.

Fear wasn't the only thing that occupied my mind, however. There was something else, something weightier that started to occupy my thoughts: a girl named Judy. The summer before I was in sixth grade, we belonged to the Beachwood Community Pool, and it was there I met the true love of my preteen life. I remember I was standing in the three-foot-deep area of the pool when a girl told me that Judy liked me and wanted to know if I would be her boyfriend. I remember considering the proposition and saying yes, even though I had never talked to her and didn't have any feelings for her yet.

But that night, I called her on the phone. We spent the next three hours talking. Mitchell and Susie were so fascinated by it they sat close to me and listened, even though they could only hear my side of the conversation. I don't know where my parents were. I think they went out. We talked about the amusement park and what rides we liked, the movies and TV shows we watched, whatever came to mind. By the end of the call I was deeply "in love." (Although I had been "in love" several times before, this was the first time I'd fallen for a girl that I'd actually had a conversation with!)

Perhaps you remember your own puppy loves. It is such an innocent, overpowering feeling. There is something very mysterious, powerful, and beautiful about it. But I also soon learned it could disappear as quickly as it came. I "went steady" with Judy for a few weeks. Then one day I rode my bicycle over to her house. I don't remember what prompted it, but she called me a little shrimp.

I told her, "If you call me that again, I'm breaking up with you."

She looked me full in the face and said, "You little shrimp."

I said, "OK, that's it!"

I was through with her. I got on my bike and rode away. My attitude was, "Fine. Her loss."

As I look back, I'm happy and thankful I had so much self-assurance. It was so easy to just walk away from her. I had no problem with it and didn't look back, even though I had been so infatuated with her the day before.

Later that afternoon, she called and apologized and asked me to be her boyfriend again. I agreed, but the relationship only lasted for a total of five weeks because my family soon moved to Pepper Pike, where I started middle school in a new school district.

Business was booming for my dad, and he wanted a house that showed it. It wasn't a mansion, but it was definitely an upgrade, and Pepper Pike was certainly a more exclusive neighborhood. It wasn't as Jewish as Beachwood, but because Jewish people stick together and there were still many Jews in Pepper Pike, I still lived in a Jewish bubble.

On the edge of my teen years this move marked not just a new chapter for my family but a new chapter for me. The grace and innocence of childhood was slowly beginning to fade, and I had the first inkling of needing to look for something more.

3

COMING OUT OF INNOCENCE

BEFORE WE LEFT Beachwood, I'd already started Hebrew school at the Conservative synagogue in preparation for my Bar Mitzvah, which would take place when I was thirteen. The classes were devoted mostly to learning how to read Hebrew texts and memorizing passages and prayers. While I was not the best student at public school, I was even worse at Hebrew school, which I felt was empty and pointless. It seemed so dry. It had nothing to do with what was going on in my life or with having a personal relationship with God, as far as I could tell.

We had a carpool set up so that three times a week my mom or one of the other kids' moms would pick us up after school and take us to the synagogue. I was so bored during the lessons that one time I decided to just walk slowly toward the entrance to the synagogue until my mom, who had dropped us off, drove away. Then, when the coast was clear, I snuck over into a small wooded area that was beside the synagogue. I hung out there and sat staring into space, looking at the few trees until the lesson was over.

When no one asked any questions or wondered where I'd been,

I went to my secluded little spot a few more times. I felt closer to God in the woods than I did in the synagogue, not that I snuck away for any kind of spiritual experience. I just did it to avoid sitting in the classes.

In the long run my sneaking away and lack of attentiveness caught up with me. About a year before my Bar Mitzvah it was painfully obvious I wasn't going to be ready, so my parents hired a private tutor to walk me through my lessons. I had to sit with that tutor all that summer until I could prove I could do everything I needed to do for my ceremony without a hitch.

You've probably heard of Bar Mitzvahs and may even have attended a ceremony. Traditionally a boy's Bar Mitzvah happens right around his thirteenth birthday and is meant to mark his coming of age to be responsible to God for himself. The celebration is described using two Hebrew words: *bar*, meaning son, and *mitzvah*, meaning commandment. Thus when you are bar mitzvahed, you become a son of the commandments. (Girls are bat mitzvahed at the age of twelve—girls being recognized as more mature and ready a year earlier. *Bat* means daughter, and thus they become a daughter of the commandments.) Religiously these ceremonies mark when young men and women become morally responsible for themselves.

My Bar Mitzvah ceremony was on Saturday, January 23, 1971—the day before my thirteenth birthday—at Park Synagogue in Cleveland, Ohio. (I still have the certificate for it on the wall in my office.) It was a momentous day. There were two of us who were supposed to be bar mitzvahed together, but the other boy wasn't ready, so I had to do it all on my own. The ceremony itself was about three hours. The entire synagogue community was invited as well as anyone my parents wanted to be present to mark the occasion.

I went to the synagogue in the morning for Shabbat service, where I led a significant portion of it and was formally bar mitzvahed. Looking back, I'm amazed at how well I remembered all the Hebrew liturgy and prayers I'd memorized for that day. I memorized sections of the Torah—the first five books of the Old Testament—and a portion from the haftarah—the writings of the prophets. I sang many of the special prayers in Hebrew. I spent a lot of time preparing, and my tutor had trained me well. I'm sure my parents were very proud. In fact, I don't know that I made any mistakes. I was so relieved when it was finally over.

Then it was party time.

My parents rented a huge room at an upscale party center for the evening celebration. We had a first-class meal, and then there was dancing, with two bands—one for the younger people and one for the older. I don't know exactly how many were there, maybe three hundred to four hundred. I was allowed to invite anyone I wanted. There was food galore and lots to drink for the adults. I think I got to have some champagne. A Bar Mitzvah is meant to be a joyful time, but mine became more and more of a big party and less and less of a religious celebration as things moved into the evening.

Me at age thirteen at my Bar Mitzvah in 1971

It was my party, so I had a great time goofing around with my friends and dancing with as many girls as I could. One funny memory I have is slow dancing with a girl I really liked at the time who was a full foot taller than I was.

I'll leave up to you what that must have looked like. But I didn't care. It was my night.

After being bar mitzvahed, it was up to me if I went to synagogue, so I didn't go unless it was a special holiday and we went as a family. It was a relief to not have Hebrew school or a tutor after school anymore. That freedom meant I could do something else with my time. I was a seventh grader that year, attending Brady Middle School in Pepper Pike. It was the year I first started wrestling. My cousin, who was several years older, had wrestled, and that inspired me to try it.

I'm sure the fact that wrestling was the one middle school sport where my smaller size did not put me at a disadvantage also had something to do with it. I started wrestling in the lightest weight class, the seventy-eight-pound division. I remember the first meet we had. My dad was in the stands. When the whistle blew, I ran over and grabbed my opponent but then wasn't sure what to do next. He did something at that point, spun me around, tossed me to the ground, and pinned me. It was over fast.

While that would discourage a lot of kids, I remember walking off the mat determined that my next match would be different. I was hooked. I'd found something I wanted to get good at and had confidence that I could. I loved it!

Looking back, I realize that I was looking to define who I was. Wrestling had a structure and demanded a discipline that made me feel secure and competent. It created boundaries and a world that was small and simple enough for me to understand. I was yearning for something to give me significance and a sense of accomplishment and identity. I felt wrestling could fulfill all of those. I was willing to give up just about anything to get better at it.

I remember that at one point my parents offered to pay for

Mitchell, Susie, and me to fly out to California and visit our aunt. I asked instead if they would pay for me to go to wrestling camp. After some discussion between them, they agreed. I went to wrestling camp, while Mitchell and Susie went to California.

By the eighth grade I was fully engaged with and all in on the sport. It made me a little cocky, which got me into trouble. There was this kid on the bus whom I made an arrogant comment to one day, and as a result, I became his archenemy. He seemed to become obsessed with wanting to harass me. My challenge was I was only about 80 pounds and he was about 120. Every day, we rode the same bus, and he would be in the back calling out, "Little Kirtie Schneider," over and over in a singsong way.

I ignored him for a while, hoping he would stop, but he didn't. After a while it really started to vex me. I remember sitting at home one day thinking, "What am I going to do? This guy is really making my life miserable." So remembering how I'd gotten the kid on my street to stop throwing rocks at me, I decided I would fight him. Despite our size difference, I made up my mind to face him.

The day after I made this decision, I got on the bus and he started in again. "Look! It's little *Kir*tie Schnei*der*, little *Kir*tie Schnei*der*..." I can still picture it. Sitting on the bus, I was wearing my new orange bell-bottom pants. I was nervous, but I had a plan, and I was going to act.

When the bus arrived at school, I got off before him, stepped to the side, and waited. As soon as he stepped down, *bam*! I hit him right in the face. Next we ended up on the ground, half wrestling, half fighting. Before either of us was able to do too much damage, one of the teachers got between us and broke it up.

The teacher marched us to the principal's office, we got a

talking-to, and then we were suspended for the rest of the day. When my dad came to get me, I felt the principal somehow quietly communicated to my dad, "Your son did the right thing in sticking up for himself." I mean, you could see this guy was almost twice my size. I felt satisfied, and that kid never picked on me again.

With that off my back, my focus returned to girls. That year, I fell "in love" with another girl I had never talked to, and I don't think she even knew I existed. I remember thinking about her day after day, enthralled with her beauty. One day I walked by her classroom door, looked inside, and felt as if I was going to faint. Seriously. I was overwhelmed, and it felt for a brief second that the life had drained from me. What makes this story even more comical is that I was the second-shortest boy in my grade and this girl was probably a third bigger than me in size. But even though I was the size of a Chihuahua, I acted like a Great Dane. The size of the girls did not intimidate me.

Somehow I think my tendency toward romance was a precursor of my pursuit to know and experience a supernatural God. I have always been drawn toward the transcendent, and these romantic infatuations were a window into a realm of mystical beauty.

Music was also very important to me in those years. Often when I listened to music on the record player in my room, it transported me; something in it would touch my soul—sometimes it was just a few notes that elicited something deep within me. It was like I'd gotten a sense of something divine. Music carried me beyond the physical notes themselves into a feeling filled with depth.

Sometimes I would play the same section of a song over and over again hundreds of times, trying to get in touch with what it was that so moved me. I would just sit in my room, pick up the record player's needle, and then carefully place it back a few grooves to listen to the section again. I remember doing this in college and driving the guys next door crazy with it, but I was chasing something. What was it that I felt when I heard those notes? What had they captured and conveyed to me that I couldn't quite grasp? I hungered to enter permanently into the mystical reality that music transported me to. Somehow I knew there was something more than what I could see right in front of me. I believed that I could experience some type of supernatural victory, freedom, and bliss.

By the time I was getting ready to enter high school, I was excited and sensed that the world was full of new and fun possibilities.

4

KIRT SCHNEIDER THE WRESTLER

I SET FOOT IN Orange High School with a growing sense of swagger.

By the end of my freshman year I started occasionally smoking cigarettes and drinking beer with my friends. Left to ourselves with more freedom than ever, my friends and I started doing crazy—and sometimes dangerous—things. One was we started making our own little homemade firecrackers (actually they weren't so little) that we'd light and leave in the street, hoping they'd blow up just as a car came by. They weren't big enough to actually damage the vehicle, but they were definitely loud enough to scare the driver half to death. (I know it was stupid, but that's what we did.) We took saltpeter, charcoal, and sulfur; crushed and mixed them all together; and then packed our mixture into pill bottles to make them like the big M-80 firecrackers that were popular at the time.

We would then put in a fuse and tape up the pill bottle real tight. We'd set these mini bombs in the street when we heard a car coming, light the fuse, then run and hide in the bushes and watch to see what would happen. Thankfully we never got the timing quite right and no one was ever hurt. We were never caught either. Eventually it grew old, and we moved on to other pranks, some of them even stupider. When I think back on some of the things I did, I still cringe, and I am very thankful for God's protection over my life during those years when I didn't know Him.

Another thing I remember doing that could have led to disaster was when my dad asked me to pull the weeds next to our driveway. Our driveway was fairly long, maybe about 150 feet, and made of asphalt, and there were weeds growing up the side of it about eighteen inches deep. It was a huge job, and I didn't want to do it. So to get the job done before my dad really got mad, I got the gasoline for my minibike out of the garage, poured it on the weeds, and then threw a match, thinking this way I could get the weeding over with quickly. Again, I was lucky I didn't set any of the trees in our front yard on fire. After this incident my dad just left all the yard work to a professional gardener. Dad was making enough money to hire people, so it was easier for him to leave it to them than to get Mitchell and me to do it right.

In some ways I think I was just a very daring kid who didn't have common sense, but in others I think I just needed boundaries. I never really found them, and I don't think that was good for my soul. I wish I had been more dependable and helped out around the house more, but it was just never demanded of Mitchell, Susie, or me. Deep inside I wanted the discipline; I wanted the boundaries. I even asked my parents to send me to military school, which they never took me up on.

In high school my closest friends were Jewish, as all my previous friends had been. The one notable exception was a kid on the wrestling team who had the reputation of being the toughest guy in school. His name was Tim, and he was of Italian background and always wore a big cross on a chain around his neck. His family was Catholic, but for him the cross wasn't a reminder of Jesus as much as an icon of his Italian-Catholic cultural heritage. He didn't talk about Jesus with me any more than I talked about Moses with him (which was not at all).

A big reason we were friends, unfortunately, was that I liked to watch how people acted around him and hoped for a fight. His friendship also meant that I, a little guy with a big mouth, had protection. We had a lot of good times together, but when he beat up a Jewish kid for no reason, I knew that something was very wrong with him—and with me. I felt guilty, and still do, that I didn't do something to try to stop it. I still hate thinking about that incident, and I truly hope and pray the person he assaulted was able to psychologically and emotionally recover.

As I inched toward my sixteenth birthday, my battles with fear were far from over. One night I went with some friends to see the movie *The Exorcist*. (If you haven't seen the film, *don't*.) It's based on the true story of a fourteen-year-old from Maryland who got possessed by the devil. Because I didn't have a relationship with God through Yeshua at the time, it scared the living daylights out of me.

When I left the theater that night, I was overwhelmed and couldn't stop dwelling on what happened to that girl—how the devil had come to possess her. I knew that a movie like that could not even have been made if the power of evil did not exist. In other words, if true, personal evil was not real, it would not enter into people's minds to create a movie like *The Exorcist*. Bottom line: I did not laugh about the movie and blow it off as a fairy tale, as many others did. I was arrested by it. How did I know the same thing wouldn't happen to me? When I got home that night,

I tried to pretend everything was fine, but when I went to bed, I lay awake until my parents fell asleep, and then I snuck into their room and slept on the floor.

I think I did that for three weeks.

That fear tormented me, however, for months. Honestly I don't know how I ever got relief from it, other than it just dissipated with time. (Now, as you may know, I am being used of the Lord to actually cast demons out of people, so praise God, things are very different for me.) Again I had never been taught that the devil was real, and yet somehow, after watching that movie, I knew he was, and that terrified me. Even when I had pretty much gotten over it, for almost two years I didn't like being in our house alone.

Despite dealing with fear, life went on, and there were many fun times to be had. After I got my license, my grandmother decided she was too old to drive, so she gave my brother and me her car. We called it the Blue Bomb. We didn't call it the Blue Bomb at first, because it was in good shape when we first got it, but after we had it for a while, it had been through enough mishaps with us that it looked far different than it did when my nana gave it to us. So it eventually became the Blue Bomb, with all its dents and scratches.

The Blue Bomb took a dent one night when some friends and I decided to investigate a field we heard was haunted. A group of us got up the courage to go there at midnight to see what would happen. We were wandering around, looking for ghosts or whatever. Something happened—I forget exactly what—and we took off running, jumped in the Blue Bomb, and tore out of there. We were driving down the road, and all of a sudden, *bam!* We hit a guardrail. We all freaked out but kept going, scared for our lives.

Mitchell eventually used the Blue Bomb as a delivery car for a restaurant called Chicken Little. He strapped on the top of it a big yellow plastic chicken that the restaurant supplied him with and drove it all over town delivering their food. What a combo! It was quite a sight—my brother driving around with a big chicken riding atop the Blue Bomb!

I think it was that same year that I took on my first entrepreneurial venture. Some friends and I wanted to go to Virginia Beach. At first my dad told me I couldn't go, then later said I could but I needed to raise the money for the trip myself. So I got serious about starting a little company that specialized in sealing asphalt, blacktop driveways. My friends and I walked around some neighborhoods with homemade fliers, handing them out, leaving them on front doors, or sticking them under doormats. It was kind of a no-brainer job—if someone wanted us to do it, we bought five-gallon buckets of sealant at the hardware store, poured it out on the driveway, spread it around with squeegees, and then taped it off for twenty-four hours so no one would drive on it until it dried.

One man in a very nice neighborhood read our flier and asked if we could widen his driveway. I thought, "Wow, I don't know. We have never widened a driveway before; we just seal them. But let's try it." My friends agreed, so I told him we could. He wanted it widened about a foot and a half. I called a cold patch company, one that delivered cold asphalt for patching rather than the hot asphalt that was used for new driveways, because I thought we had a better chance of doing the job with the cold patch asphalt. The truck came and dumped in front of his house however many tons we'd ordered. I hired four guys from my high school to dig a trench that extended eighteen inches out along the side of his existing driveway and about a foot deep, and then had them fill it with the cold patch that the asphalt company had delivered.

Next, we rolled it out by hand, compressing it with big lawn rollers you fill with water that weigh a couple hundred pounds. By the time we were done, it looked pretty good, and we were paid.

We went to Virginia Beach and had a unique and crazy time, but I had a call from the homeowner when we got back. The extension had continued to sink and never dried right. I tried to encourage him to let it sit longer before driving on it, but when I drove past his house a month later, he'd had a professional company come in to fix it. They had to redo the whole driveway with hot asphalt rather than the cold asphalt patch my friends and I had tried. That's when I learned my first lesson about not biting off more than I could chew. That was also the end of our little business. I had every intention of doing a good job, but sometimes good intentions are not enough.

When I returned to school in the fall, wrestling continued to be the most important activity to me. I had so much of myself wrapped up in it. I also remember deeply wanting my coach to put his arm around me and call me "Son." It was not something I processed logically; it was just a deep cry in my soul. This changed, though, when I wrestled the team captain's little brother to win the varsity spot. We wrestled off, and I beat him fair and square, but his brother protested to the coach that I had won because I was awarded a penalty point. He angrily cried, "Are you going to let him win on a penalty point?" The next day, the coach gave in and made us wrestle the match over again. Looking back now, I believe I see more clearly the anti-Semitism I was up against. I lost the rematch and my varsity spot. After that my feelings for my coach soured. Subsequently that kid went on to be the Ohio state champion his junior year.

The next summer, my best friend, Steve, moved to San Diego,

California. His dad had purchased a Zip's Ice Cream Sundae Place franchise there. I'm not sure why—it wasn't like I didn't have other close friends—but losing my best friend triggered something in me. It was like a switch was flipped. Feeling slightly adrift, I made the determination to pour myself all the more into wrestling, and I became 100 percent focused on becoming an Ohio state wrestling champion in my weight class, which was a whopping ninety-eight pounds.

I started going to the YMCA in East Cleveland for its Wednesday night wrestling scrimmages, even though it was still summertime. Once the school year started, I ran almost every day of the week. My wrestling focus shut almost everything else out. I made a chart and used it year-round to keep track of my workouts and diet during the season. I faithfully kept track of each time I lifted weights, each time I ran, everything. I became like a professional athlete, training all year long.

No one else I knew of was doing that. I thought that I was going to be state champ simply because I worked harder than anybody else. It really did become my life. People thought of me as "Kirt Schneider the wrestler." I wore a leather cord around my neck with a medallion of a wrestler on it. Being a good wrestler became my identity. I envisioned myself winning the state championship and then just basking in the glory, enjoying that accomplishment, and being completely at peace for the rest of my life.

I would put a record on my turntable and lie in bed listening to the music and envisioning myself with my hand raised after winning the championship match in St. John Arena at Ohio State University, where they held the state tournament every year. It would send chills through my body.

Kirt Schneider grabs a leg as he attempts to put a move on his opponent. He won 2-0, but the team lost to Kenston 20-35.

During high school I was known as "Kirt Schneider the wrestler." Back then wrestling was my life—and sadly, it became my identity.

In eleventh grade I lost twenty-two pounds to wrestle in the 105-pound weight division.

Running through the Orange High School banner before a wrestling match was always a thrill. In those days all I wanted was to become an Ohio state wrestling champion.

I (third from left) had some good times with my friends in high school.

5

MY WORLD CRASHES

A S MY ELEVENTH-GRADE year of wrestling came around, I had to ascend a big mountain. I was about 126 pounds, and I had decided I was going to wrestle in the 105-pound weight class. I didn't have much fat; I was already just muscle and bone. At that point, my life was completely disciplined for one purpose—becoming an Ohio state champion. Dieting, exercising, and wrestling were my life. I started eating very little other than flounder because it was high in protein and had almost no fat. By the time the first day of practice rolled around, I'd already lost more than twenty pounds and weighed in at 105, exactly on weight. I didn't know anyone who had done the same or was as disciplined as I was. As I said, even though I had no formal doctrinal lens through which I approached God, I had a simple, strong, childlike faith in Him, and I believed God was going to make me the state champ because I deserved to be. I had worked harder than anybody else.

Unfortunately, psychologically I needed to win so badly it worked against me. Wrestling matches in high school consist of three rounds (also called periods) that are two minutes each, with a very short break between them. I'd go out in the first period, win, get ahead, and then think, "I'm winning; all I have to do is to keep my lead." Then, rather than continuing to wrestle offensively for the second and third periods, I would focus on keeping my advantage. Instead of continuing to wrestle offensively to win, I would start to wrestle defensively, just trying to hang on to my lead to keep from losing. This fear-based strategy caused me to lose about half my matches.

It really messed me up. I think I won maybe one more match than I lost that year. I was used to winning almost every match, but my junior year my record was something like ten wins and nine losses. The disparity between what I knew I could do and what I actually did frustrated me and pushed me to work all the harder my senior year.

I truly felt that if I wasn't going to be the best, life wasn't worth living. It wasn't that I was depressed or going to take my own life. I just had the attitude that I was going to be the best and there were no other options worth living for. I don't know where I developed that mindset, but that was truly how I thought. Simultaneously, as I was approaching eighteen years old, I realized that soon I would be leaving home, going to college, and on my own. I would be entering a world that was much larger than my wrestling universe. I knew this world outside of wrestling was larger than me, and I couldn't control it. That made me fearful. It wasn't anything overt, just a looming, internal fear at the back of my mind that I did my best to ignore. I had been burying myself in wrestling partly to escape these larger realities of life that frightened me.

For example, I remember hearing about a fifteen-year-old kid who developed cancer and died. How did I know that wouldn't happen to me? I read about a seventeen-year-old who was killed in a car accident. While that probably wasn't going to happen to me, how did I know for sure? Or how did I know something else wasn't going to go wrong? Seeing that my parents, teachers, and other authorities weren't the perfect people I thought they were when I was younger and that they didn't have all the answers contributed to my insecurity and made me feel confused about the future. I felt vulnerable and subconsciously tried to bury the feeling by throwing myself into my training all the harder. By the time I was seventeen years old, the only time I truly experienced peace of mind was when I was training or competing during wrestling season. I blocked everything else out of my mind in order to feel safe.

Going into my senior-year wrestling season, I was very confident again. In the weeks leading to our first match, we sometimes scrimmaged with a private school that was nearby, and I always wrestled the same guy. I could easily manhandle him. He was like a noodle to me. I could do any move I wanted and flip and pin him at will. As it turned out, that school was one of the first meets for the year, and I was slated to wrestle this same guy. To say that I was confident would be an understatement.

We shook hands and took our positions across from each other, and the whistle blew to start the match. We circled for a few seconds, then I shot a takedown, took him to the mat, and turned him for some back points. By the end of the first round, he had wrestled as usual, and I was way, way ahead. Then I went back into my self-defeating pattern. I went into defense mode again, just trying to get through the match with my lead intact. At the end of the second round the score was closer, but I was still ahead. Into the third round I had control, but then he got a reversal, and before I knew it, the buzzer sounded, ending the match. I looked up, and he had edged one point ahead of me. His bench went crazy. The referee grabbed both of our arms, and then raised his as the winner.

I wanted to die.

I went back to our sideline, sat, and dropped my head into my hands. I was so disgusted, so sick and tired of myself. I had just done the same thing I had my entire junior season and had now lost to someone I knew beyond the shadow of a doubt I could beat! It was unbelievable.

As it happened, that was a Friday night, and we had a tournament the very next day. A guy in my weight class who would also be there had placed well in the high-level district competition the year before and was looking to contend for the state title that year. He was one of the best wrestlers at the tournament. Going into my match with him, I decided to hold nothing back. It was a new beginning. I wrestled aggressively to win, not just for the first period but for all three periods—the whole time. This time, when the referee took our arms at the end of the match, it was mine he raised. I beat him!

I was elated all the way home. During the bus ride back, the coach took a few minutes to talk about the overall team effort; then he announced that I was the wrestler of the week. That meant I won what we called the pizza prize, because the winner got a certificate for a free pizza.

I remember getting off the bus, going to my car, starting the engine, and pushing in a tape by the Eagles. They launched into one of my favorite songs from the album *One of These Nights*. I turned the volume up, and I was transported. I can only describe the feeling that enveloped me as overwhelming ecstasy. It was the most incredible moment of my life up to that point. I believe I experienced the glory of God, though I would not have been able to articulate it in those words at the time. I believe that God visited me in that moment for reasons only He understands. It was unexpected and completely fulfilling.

Everything in that moment was crystal clear. The music sounded more alive than any music I had ever heard before. I was one with the music, and the music seemed to be spirit. It was transcendent. I don't really have words to describe it adequately. What I experienced in that moment I will never forget. From then on I knew I was on my way. I didn't feel there was anybody I couldn't beat. I wrestled strong, consistently winning my matches for the rest of the regular season, and held onto my dream of being the Ohio state wrestling champion at 119 pounds.

It was not to be, however. My last match of the year was in a tournament called sectionals that led up to the state championships. Bottom line, I didn't make it out of sectionals. When I walked out of the gym after wrestling that last high school match, I felt like the ground had been pulled out from underneath my feet. In that minute, all the world was drained of color. Everything I'd built my identity on was gone in an instant. I was lost and adrift. Everything I'd hoped for was now out of reach.

I had a great girlfriend at the time whom I'd been going steady with for about three months. We were very close. Suddenly I felt like I didn't know her anymore. I felt disconnected from everyone whom I had felt close to just the day before. In fact, I felt completely alone and estranged from every single human being on the planet.

When my mom looked me in the eye, I wasn't able to meet her gaze. A week or so later my girlfriend and I broke up. I was incapable of being in relationship with anyone because suddenly I had no sense of identity, purpose, or destiny since it had all been tied to wrestling. Now that I no longer had wrestling, the world I had known came to a very abrupt end.

When I told my parents about feeling aimless and the fear I was experiencing, they said, "Why don't you go see a counselor?" So they took me to see this counselor, and he told me, "You just need to run (as in exercise). It will slow down your thoughts." So I started running, but it didn't help. So they took me to see a psychiatrist. He told me that my problem was my father—that I needed to "overcome my father." I was never really sure what he meant by that. I didn't know what to do with what he was telling me.

In addition, for the first time in my life, my physical size started to bother me. Up to that point, amazingly enough, it didn't. I was always brimming with confidence, even though I was only five feet five and a half (as I still am today). I had always assumed I would shoot up like my cousins, who were all over six feet. Now that I was past my growing years—and still only five feet five and a half—another foundation of my identity had been cut down. My parents even took me to a doctor to try to get growth hormone pills for me, but the doctor said, "I'm sorry; there's no room left in your bones to grow." I was small and going to stay that way.

I didn't have confidence in myself academically either, because I'd never put any effort into school. I thought it wouldn't matter. I didn't care. I was a partier. I had my girlfriends; school wasn't important. Now, all of a sudden, my poor study habits were a huge handicap. Most of my friends were serious about what they wanted to do in life and saw good grades as important to where they wanted to go. I didn't. I hadn't focused on a life beyond wrestling since I believed that once I became a state champ, I would have climbed to the top of the mountain and would then spend the rest of my life basking in the glory. But now that my mountain had come crumbling down all around me, I was utterly lost.

When I wrestled, I felt like I was bigger than the world, but when wrestling ended, I very abruptly realized I wasn't. I realized that I was at the mercy of the world around me and there were no barriers to protect me from whatever I feared. Life was a lot bigger than people who wrestled 119 pounds, and I couldn't hide in the microcosm of wrestling anymore.

Kirt Schneider, the wrestler, was gone. Even though I ended up getting a small wrestling scholarship to the University of Tampa, financial constraints forced the university to drop their wrestling program. All my cool and swagger evaporated. I began a life of just going through the motions, hoping against hope that I'd find something to hope for again, something that would give my life the meaning that wrestling had. I was desperately trying to overcome my insecurities and the sense of vulnerability I felt.

At the same time, I still had this feeling that there was something glorious to find. I knew there was something worth living for; I just didn't know what it was. My life didn't have to be empty and filled with fear. There was purpose in the universe. I knew it existed.

But how and where was I ever going to find it?

6

LOST

O NCE IN FLORIDA at the University of Tampa, I found myself in a place that was miles away from my home and living in a state of paranoia. I began sleeping as much as possible in an attempt to avoid the emotional darkness. I didn't know how else to deal with it.

No longer having an anchor or a clear sense of who I was, I felt vulnerable to any fear that might pop in my head. I'd get thoughts such as, "What if I were thrown in jail and got raped?" Even though I really had no reason to think I would get thrown in jail, such thoughts sent me reeling. What would I do? I had no protection. I had no solid ground on which to stand and was therefore emotionally vulnerable to all kinds of defiled and destructive thoughts.

It was sometime during these years that I had another fear grip me. Since early in my teens, I'd owned pornographic magazines and looked at them regularly. I think it just seemed like natural sexual exploration to my parents since they never said anything to me about them. I had them tucked away in my bathroom cabinet. This particular time, I opened a magazine to a picture of a man and woman having sex. I'd looked at the same image many times before, but for some reason this time the image of the man jumped out at me. I'd never really noticed him before, and when I did, it sent chills through me. The sexuality of this greasy man came over me and seemed to possess me. The alarming thought came to my mind, "What if you're a homosexual?"

I had always been extremely attracted to girls, as I've already shared. But when this happened to me, I was gripped with fear. My identity and sense of self was so fragile that this thought plagued me for the next couple of years. It was another example of a power greater than me that was overcoming me and then causing me to become something I didn't want to be or do something I didn't want to do, like jumping off the boat or driving my car into the side rail, as I wrote about earlier. It wasn't a desire but a fear that took possession of me and was overwhelming.

During this time, I could feel evil hovering over me when I'd lie down to sleep at night, laughing at me and somehow causing me to agree with it against myself. At the time, I had no biblical knowledge about the devil, but somehow I could feel and sense him sadistically laughing over me. I could palpably feel him hovering on top of me. Now, looking back, I realize that what I experienced was a personal attack from the realm of evil on my personhood and destiny. It was utter torment, and it wasn't until Messiah Jesus revealed Himself to me at the age of twenty that I was set free from this nightmare of fear.

While dealing with this, I continued to take classes at the University of Tampa, but I saw no reason to return in the fall. The next year, I transferred to Ohio State University so I could be closer to home. Steve, my old high school friend who'd moved away to San Diego, was attending Ohio State, and we decided to room together. I hoped maybe that would return some normalcy to my life. Steve and I pledged the same Jewish fraternity. Being the prankster and individualist I was, I got it into my head that I would start my own fraternity within this official fraternity and be the president of it. I gave out homemade pins to the guys I asked to join me. The established leadership of the fraternity was none too happy about my little mutiny. I'm surprised I didn't get kicked out. Instead they commanded me to shovel their driveway every morning that winter. This punishment didn't last long because I soon dropped out of school to open a discotheque.

I just sort of existed, floating through life without direction or intent. I partied, trying to take the edge off my fears. I wanted back the feeling of purpose wrestling had given me, the bliss I'd felt sitting in my car listening to the Eagles the day I had my wrestling breakthrough. I pondered, "What can I do to get that feeling back? What can I do to feel better?" I had no idea. There was nothing that excited me at all.

I thought about becoming a lawyer. Lawyers did important work and made good money. But in the back of my mind I was thinking, "What will happen when you're sixty-five and retire from law? You're going to go through the same thing you are dealing with now. Your identity will be lost, just like it was when wrestling ended." If I built my life on practicing law, the same thing was going to happen when my career ended and I retired. I'd be left wondering what I would do with the rest of my life. Who would I be when I no longer was an attorney? I realized I needed to build my identity on something more permanent than a career, but I didn't know what that something was. It would take me time to realize I needed a spiritual solution.

You see, in all of this I never considered God might be the answer I was looking for, because I was never taught that God could satisfy, that He was personal, and that He loved me individually and specifically. I just had a sense that I needed something more. So I kept searching.

My thoughts returned to the idea of making some money. I knew it wasn't really the answer, because I saw that people who had money still had problems. (There was divorce and infidelity in Pepper Pike just like anywhere else; some even fell prey to organized crime, trying to get ahead.) I knew money wouldn't be a cure to my troubles, but grasping at straws, I hoped it would make me feel better.

In the winter of 1977 the movie *Saturday Night Fever* had just come out, helping kick off the disco craze. People were lining up for blocks to get into discotheques. I thought maybe I could find a good location and open my own, so I dropped out of Ohio State at winter break in hopes of becoming an entrepreneur and opening a discotheque.

My plan was to get friends of the family to be investors, and then I'd become a part owner and run the club. My first step was to earn some money to travel to find the perfect location. I knew I would need a solid business plan to attract investors, and that plan would have to start with the right location. My thinking was pretty simplistic, I admit, but I wasn't even twenty years old yet, an age when—as you may remember—a certain degree of naivete and foolish optimism at what we can accomplish goes with the territory.

So I got a job selling encyclopedias door to door for P. F. Collier & Son in order to get the finances I needed to travel around the country to find the right location for the discotheque. As things turned out, I was a pretty good salesman, and I rose up through the ranks quickly. By the summer of 1978 the company had asked me to be a sales manager.

I was assigned a team I was responsible to train, and I would drive them in my van to different locations every day to canvass the neighborhoods. I'd drop my team off in the afternoon and pick them up around 9:30 p.m. I got a commission off whatever they sold as well as a larger commission off whatever sales I could make. Door-to-door sales was a hard job for many, but I was good at it.

The company had meetings for us as managers to brainstorm together and to receive training. There were five sales managers in our area east of Cleveland. I usually got to these meetings a little early, and one night I got into a discussion with one of the other managers who arrived early as well. He was really excited about a new book he was reading, so I asked him about it. It was *Autobiography of a Yogi*, written by an Indian guru named Paramahansa Yogananda. The stories he told me about this man captured my imagination. He told me this guru could fight tigers with his bare hands and enter into a meditative state that so transcended the natural world he would levitate off of the ground.

I remember thinking how cool it would be if I could do that! The more he told me about the book, the more it fascinated me. A day or so later I went to a bookstore and bought my own copy. It was the first book I ever bought with my own money. As soon as I got home, I started reading it and flipping through the pictures. It felt like I had found my new "wrestling"!

Sometimes people have a hard time believing I fell so hard for what was in this book because it was unbiblical, but you have to realize just how spiritually naive and illiterate I was. The teaching I had in preparing for my Bar Mitzvah mentioned God, of course, but not a God we could have a personal relationship with. We didn't really discuss whether the miracles of

Moses were real. Our job was to learn to read Hebrew and memorize the prayers. It was a cultural indoctrination, not a spiritual journey.

I had always known on the inside that there was something more. I sensed spirituality was real, but I had no framework for *truth*—or revelation that there was an evil out there masquerading as truth. All interpretations of spiritual truth sort of melded together for me. The miracles of Paramahansa Yogananda touched that sense of wonder I believed in. I prayed a simple prayer in my heart: "God, if this is real, if this guy can really levitate off the ground, I've found my new purpose in life. This is what I want to do."

As far as I was concerned, finding this book was an attempt by God to make Himself known to me. I was looking for something more, and suddenly here it was finding me! As I read the book, I thought I'd found a reality higher than making money, something that would not end as wrestling had or a career would. If I got to a place where I could levitate off the ground, I thought I would have arrived and my life would be bliss.

I was all in.

I read the book every night after I got home from selling encyclopedias. In the book was the address of Paramahansa Yogananda's temple in Los Angeles, and I decided I needed to go there. I asked for vacation time at work, packed my things in my van, and was off across the country to Los Angeles to study the yogi's teachings.

On my way, not far out of Cleveland, I stopped to pick up some hitchhikers who were headed to Philadelphia to see a different Indian guru called Guru Maharaj Ji. I was intrigued by my new traveling mates' stories. I said to myself, "Listen, you're on your way to Paramahansa Yogananda's temple in Los Angles.

Why not go to Philadelphia first to check this guru out?" So I agreed to take them all the way to Philadelphia.

When we got to Philadelphia, we entered a large auditorium with hundreds of people. Guru Maharaj Ji was set up on the stage, sitting on a golden throne. Despite my openness, it struck me as creepy and weird, so before too long I got back in my van and continued on to the temple in Los Angeles. When I got there, nothing much was going on. It was in a peaceful setting that was well landscaped, and there were a few people just kind of walking around outside. I could not detect any organized way to get involved. I found no reception desk or information center about classes or programs. So after my very long drive from Cleveland to Los Angeles, I ended up only hanging out there for a day. Then I got back in my gray van and headed back to Cleveland. Interestingly enough I wasn't discouraged by this.

When I returned to Cleveland, I erected a little new age shrine made of colored bedsheets in my bedroom. I'd sit in it, trying to meditate and find my third eye (a new age term I'd picked up from Paramahansa Yogananda's book).[1]

No one seemed to think this was a dangerous path for my life. Nor did anyone react like this was something I needed to be saved from because it contradicted the Hebrew Scriptures. This was because most of the Jews I knew were secular and because many young Jewish people were involved in the New Age in the sixties and seventies. They didn't see it as conflicting with the Jewish faith or endangering my soul.

No one, I guess, except, as it turned out, Jesus Himself.

I remember the day everything dramatically changed. It was a hot August night in 1978. I was in the midst of my quest to be able to levitate off the ground. I was twenty years old and still selling encyclopedias door-to-door. I started the day telling myself, "I'm going to be as nice as I can to everybody I meet today." It felt like such a pure, almost divine impulse. I was resolute. No matter how many doors were slammed in my face, I was going to be as kind to others as I knew how to be. I was on a spiritual mission.

I started off well, but as the day wore on, I developed a headache. Then the headache grew worse and worse. It turned into the worst headache I can ever remember having. Once I got done selling encyclopedias for the day, I drove to a bar called, believe it or not, the Lion and Lamb and got a beer, but my headache was so bad I couldn't finish it. I gave up and went home to go to bed. I fell right to sleep.

Then in the middle of the night I was awakened into a state of supernatural conscious awareness. All of my senses were heightened, and then I had a vision. I can still see it clearly in my mind's eye. In that state, Jesus appeared on the cross. A ray of red light came out of heaven and beamed down on His head. There was a group of people looking at Him from a distance. I could see the terrain in which the cross was staked. It felt as if I were actually there, witnessing the crucifixion—like I had been transported back in time two thousand years.

I knew the light was coming from God because it was coming from straight above, right through the sky. I also knew the person on the cross was Jesus. As I looked on Him, I knew that God was telling me that He knew me and that Jesus was the way to know Him.

Nothing was spoken. I heard no divine voice or audible words. I don't think the entire experience lasted more than a second or two, but it marked me. In that moment, I realized I didn't have to be afraid anymore. There was a way out of the paranoia I'd been experiencing; there was an answer to all the horror that had assaulted my mind. I had nothing to fear. God was with me and had a plan for my life. In Jesus I knew I would overcome and find my purpose and destiny.

That night, my life changed forever. I knew within my deepest being that Jesus was the way to God and that I would have victory in Him.

I want you to think about this: No one witnessed to me—never in my life had anybody shared the gospel with me. I had never read the New Testament. Jesus was as far away from my existence as the man on the moon. I never thought about Jesus. I had never considered Jesus. He was a nonissue for me. I was a Jew. Jesus was foreign; He was for non-Jews. But the God of my forefathers—Abraham, Isaac, and Jacob—revealed Himself to me, showing me that Jesus was the Messiah and "the way, and the truth, and the life" (John 14:6).

Immediately after the vision I looked at my clock radio. It was 3:30 a.m. I went to the restroom and then back to bed. I pulled the covers over me and fell into a deep sleep. In the morning, the headache I'd had was gone without a trace.

Everything had changed.

Hope had come into my heart. It was—and still is—the greatest breakthrough I've experienced in my life. In an instant I realized I could be free. The fact that the ray of light came down from heaven caused me to recognize that regardless of what I was facing, I could transcend it. I now had a new confidence from the heavenly realm.

I had become so defeated after wrestling ended that I could not even look people in the eyes. But when Jesus revealed Himself to me, I began to force myself to look up again. God had broken into my world, and I found myself now standing on a foundation from which I could begin to rebuild my life. He became my center. I was determined I was going to move upward in Him from then on.

This doesn't mean that all of a sudden my life became easy. I still had a tremendous amount of personal work to do within myself, but somehow I knew that through Jesus I would overcome.

I was very excited. I started telling everybody about what had happened to me and what I had seen. I told my mom, my brother, my sister, my dad. I had found my answer, and God had revealed to me that it was Jesus.

I had no idea what I was in for.

7

WHEN A JEW FINDS JESUS

A s I SHARED previously, Jesus had always been a nonissue in our house when I was growing up. We never talked about Him, just like we didn't talk about Mars or Martians because they were not part of our universe. But it was more than that, although I didn't know it at the time. There was a reason we didn't talk about Jesus, and it wasn't just that He wasn't part of our world—He was actually an enemy of our world, at least in the minds of my ancestors.

My grandparents had left Europe because of persecution—persecution at the hands of Christians who thought of Jews as "Christ killers." Christianity wasn't just another religion; it was a *persecuting* religion. Hitler's picture had hung on the walls of churches in Germany before and during World War II. Christians had been the bulk of the mobs that had smashed the windows of Jewish shopkeepers and set fire to synagogues on Kristallnacht, the night anti-Semites took to the streets in Germany, a first step toward the concentration camps of the Holocaust.

Many of the Germans who put Jews in death camps were Christians in name. (Christians such as Corrie ten Boom who loved the Jewish people were far from the rule.) Though it was unspoken, as far as many Jews were concerned, Jesus and Hitler were cut from the same cloth. I was very naive about all of this because my parents never talked about their pasts or anti-Semitism and because I had experienced very few anti-Semitic attitudes against myself (although looking back now, I can see some things that I couldn't see then). Remember, I grew up in Jewish communities, so I was surrounded by Jews, not anti-Semites.

I had no idea that day, but most in our community saw becoming a believer in Jesus as becoming a traitor to the Jewish people.

It's difficult to understand how deeply this runs. There isn't anything a Jew can believe that will make him or her a non-Jew in the eyes of the larger Jewish community, except for becoming a believer in Jesus. You can be an atheist and still be considered a Jew. For example, I have an atheist uncle who was invited to speak at a close family member's Bat Mitzvah, but the officiating rabbi would not allow me to participate in the ceremony because of my faith in Jesus. Jews who believe in Jesus are put out of the synagogue, just as it was in Yeshua's day (John 9:22; 16:2). You can be agnostic and still be Jewish; you can be deeply involved in the New Age and still be Jewish. You can even be a Buddhist and still be considered Jewish. Yet a line is drawn when it comes to Jesus. There is a very subtle sense within the Jewish community that to be a good Jew, you have to *reject* a Jew who believes in Jesus.

In fact, any Jew can make *aliyah* to Israel. *Aliyah* means "going up" in Hebrew.[1] Metaphorically, making *aliyah* means one moves to the Promised Land and becomes an Israeli citizen. No matter where a Jew is from or what he or she believes, the person is granted citizenship. At the time of this writing, any Jew could make *aliyah* with one exception: those who have changed their religion. This often includes Jews who believe in Jesus. The governing rabbis in Israel, along with the government they exert control over, have determined that a Jew who believes in Jesus in no longer a Jew but has converted to Christianity, another religion, and therefore has no right to Israeli citizenship. (I could educate more here, but in a nutshell this goes all the way back to the religious leaders of Jesus' day. The mindset of the Pharisees who rejected Jesus [Yeshua in Hebrew] has been passed on to every succeeding generation of Jews since. In fact, the Pharisees of Yeshua's day are the origin of today's Orthodox Rabbinic Judaism.) Even Russian Jews, for example, who know very little about God or Judaism because they were raised under atheistic communism, are granted citizenship, despite only being biologically Jewish. But Jews who believe Jesus is the Messiah are not welcome to make their home in Israel. It is not logical.

Of course I did not understand this when I started talking to my family about Jesus. Again I don't remember Jesus coming up even once in my family through all my years growing up. But now, without fully realizing it, I had just placed a huge wedge between me and my family, and the more I spoke with them about my Messiah, the deeper the divide became. Since I identify with Yeshua as much as I do, I cannot compartmentalize my faith and beliefs. Yeshua is my center. As a result I am looked down upon, rejected, and despised as the odd man out. Since the day I gave my life to Jesus, I have not been able to have a deep relationship with my own flesh-and-blood relatives—it has been this way for over forty years now. To continue relationship with my family would mean never sharing my experiences of Jesus or discussing Him, and that is something I am unwilling to do.

Despite my being rejected, my Jewish identity is so much stronger now as a believer in Yeshua than it ever was before I knew Him. I don't identify at all with the concept that I've lost my Jewishness because I follow Yeshua. Instead God has clarified my Jewish identity. Yeshua is the Messiah, and as a Jewish believer who follows Him, I've experienced some of the same rejection He did.

It all comes down to this: either Yeshua is who He said He is or He isn't. If He is, then any Jew who follows Him is a true Jew, a Jew in the fullest sense of the word. If Yeshua isn't the Messiah, then I am an enemy of my people, demonically deceived, and have put my hope in a lie.

> And if Christ has not been raised, then our preaching is vain, your faith also is vain. Moreover we are even found to be false witnesses of God, because we testified against God that He raised Christ, whom He did not raise, if in fact the dead are not raised. For if the dead are not raised, not even Christ has been raised; and if Christ has not been raised, your faith is worthless; you are still in your sins. Then those also who have fallen asleep in Christ have perished. If we have hoped in Christ in this life only, we are of all men most to be pitied. But now Christ has been raised from the dead, the first fruits of those who are asleep.
>
> —1 CORINTHIANS 15:14–20

I have risked and staked my life and Jewish identity on the resurrection of Jesus, which confirms that He is the Messiah. For me, however, my primary identity is not being Jewish. My primary identity is that I have been chosen by Father God in Messiah Yeshua. I am very blessed to be Jewish, but there is something beyond this. I identify with Paul's words:

Blessed be the God and Father of our Lord Jesus Christ, who...
chose us in Him before the foundation of the world, that we
would be holy and blameless before Him. In love He predes-
tined us to adoption as sons through Jesus Christ to Himself,
according to the kind intention of His will.

—EPHESIANS 1:3–5

For we are the true circumcision, who worship in the Spirit of
God and glory in Christ Jesus and put no confidence in the
flesh, although I myself might have confidence even in the
flesh. If anyone else has a mind to put confidence in the flesh,
I far more: circumcised the eighth day, of the nation of Israel,
of the tribe of Benjamin, a Hebrew of Hebrews; as to the Law,
a Pharisee; as to zeal, a persecutor of the church; as to the
righteousness which is in the Law, found blameless.

But whatever things were gain to me, those things I have
counted as loss for the sake of Christ. More than that, I count
all things to be loss in view of the surpassing value of knowing
Christ Jesus my Lord, for whom I have suffered the loss of all
things, and count them but rubbish so that I may gain Christ.

—PHILIPPIANS 3:3–8

For a Jew, going down this road called "the Way" in the New
Testament (Acts 9:2) requires letting go of being esteemed as
Jewish by family and community. This is a road that few Jews
will choose. Their primary identity is being Jewish. Most want
only truth that will affirm their Jewish identity. So for most of
the Jewish people I have known, community and identity are
more important than God. To consider Jesus requires giving up
too much of themselves. It is too painful.

Regardless of the cost, though, my vision of Jesus had so
impacted me that I couldn't stop talking about it, and I shared
it with everybody. Eventually someone I shared my experience
with suggested I get a New Testament and start reading it. So I

did. It wasn't until then that I learned that Jesus was very different from the Yogi Paramahansa Yogananda. I had thought it was all the same. I even thought the vision of Jesus had actually come because I was opening up to spiritual things through the Yogi's autobiography and should therefore continue down the path of the guru. Again, I was scripturally illiterate.

But when I started reading the Bible, the words were like fire coming off the page to me. I was drawn to them like a moth to a flame. I would go up to my dad and say, "Dad, look at this verse: 'that God was in Christ reconciling the world to Himself!'" (See 2 Corinthians 5:19.) I thought God's Word was so cool. I hoped when I shared it, it would mean the same to him as it did to me. I opened the Bible to John 1 and shared verses 1 and 14 with my brother. "Look at this, Mitchell. 'In the beginning was the Word, and the Word was with God, and the Word was God. And the Word became flesh.' Isn't this mind-blowing and amazing?" I thought they would see what God had shown me, but it didn't play out like that. Instead my zeal put them in a state of panic and alarm.

At first, though, my family didn't really react. It was just too shocking to register. I'm sure they hoped it was a phase that was going to pass. But as time went on and I kept talking about Jesus, my parents became more and more worried. Something crazy had gotten a hold of their son!

While I was oblivious to it at the time, I know now that my parents felt a lot of shame to have their eldest son walking around the Jewish community in Cleveland, telling everybody about Jesus. I was too emotionally immature and wrapped up in my own struggles to realize how what had happened to me affected them. They began to think someone had brainwashed me. They were also concerned that I had gone nuts. (In Yiddish you would say *mashugana*, meaning crazy.)

While my parents' concerns grew, my hunger for Jesus grew even more. I devoured the Gospels and books of the New Testament as the bread of life. As I delved into the New Testament, I realized that the Yogi's teachings were wrong. It wasn't too long before I threw away his autobiography and disassembled and tossed out the new age temple I had built in my room.

Eventually another acquaintance said, "You should start going to church." I was so zealous that I didn't just go to one church. I started going to meetings all over the city: Baptist, Assemblies of God, nondenominational, any place that was teaching the Bible. Congregations where most of the attendees were senior citizens (at least they seemed to be seniors to me at the time; I was only twenty years old, so in reality they may have averaged no more than fifty-five years old), young peoples' meetings, Messianic services—you name it, I was there. I was on a quest to know God.

Another thing that sticks out in my mind from those early days of being a new believer is how God was working in my life to deliver me from the power of darkness. It's hard to explain. I remember going into a drugstore to pick out a card for somebody. I saw a card with a purple background, and it stunned me. I remember looking at the card and saying to myself, "Wow." Some people might describe the way I felt by saying the sky was bluer or the grass was greener. For me it was as if I was seeing color again for the first time since I was eighteen. (I was twenty-four years old at this point.) I could have told you the card was purple during the years before, but it would have appeared just as a one-dimensional color to me. Now it was like I was seeing color in a three-dimensional way—it was life-giving color. It was like the color I saw as a child. It was fresh, vibrant, and living.

The only word that came to mind was, "Wow." In that moment, I knew I had been released from the darkness that had come upon me when wrestling ended. I was stunned.

I don't want to paint this to sound magical, though. It might seem like an instantaneous change took place in my life, but while my awareness of Jesus went from night to day, my life changed much more slowly. I still had a lot of spiritual work to do.

For example, one area that changed slowly was my concept of morality. I was still largely the partier I had been in college. I was also a heavy smoker. Whenever I felt unsatisfied, I'd reach for a cigarette. I still had my porn magazines. When I met Cynthia, whom I would marry and who came from a very morally conservative background, many of my outward habits had not yet changed, even though it had been about four years since my vision. For our first date I took her to a convenience store and bought a six-pack of beer. Then I took her to a Christian coffeehouse but sat in the car and drank several of the beers first. Once I started to feel a little buzz, we went in, and it never occurred to me that somebody would question my behavior. Drinking in moderation is very much a part of the Jewish religious culture. I had very little idea of what the appropriate behavior was in this new culture and circle I was becoming a part of.

I was in love with God, full of passion, and running after Him, but I was definitely a diamond in the rough and a horse that needed to be tamed.

8

THE SPIRIT AND THE DARKNESS

GOD CONTINUED TO reach out to me. He made His Word alive to me as I read it. I learned something new every time I attended a church service or Bible study. And from time to time I continued to have Spirit-breathed dreams and experiences through which God instilled some new truth into me.

For example, shortly after my initial vision of Jesus on the cross, I had a second major experience of this type. One night in my sleep I literally saw into the spirit world. It was not a dream. I saw two spirits. One was of pure, white life. It was shaped like an egg—it was like a living egg made up of pure living spirit. It was difficult to tell how big it was. To the best of my perception, it was about three feet long and maybe a foot and a half high. It was not one-dimensional. It wasn't static but continuously in motion. It wasn't *like* life; it *was* life: "But whoever drinks of the water that I will give him shall never thirst; but the water that I will give him will become in him a well of water springing up to eternal life" (John 4:14).

All around this bright, egg-shaped swirl of life was a spirit of darkness. It was not just darkness that is the absence of light. No, this darkness was alive, and it was in motion as well. The motion of the darkness was chaotic, creepy, and random. The darkness had substance and texture to it. And while the spirit of life was sealed and self-contained, the darkness was everywhere the life wasn't. There was symmetry to how the spirit of white life moved. It had an internal coordination of movement that somehow reminded me of a friend of mine from high school. He was the most coordinated athlete I knew, and when he danced, it was like art in motion. The darkness, on the other hand, was disordered and evoked a sense of foreboding.

After God allowed me to see into the spirit realm, I prayed for revelation of what I saw that night, and I am still praying for a complete understanding. The first deep insight I received came while I was watching a movie on television. As a horrific event was about to unfold in this movie, ominous music began to play. When I heard the music, I realized it was literally a musical manifestation of the darkness I saw in that encounter. It was as if the darkness became music. Hollywood producers know exactly what type of music to play in their movies to instill fear and accentuate whatever evil event is about to unfold.

Through this revelation I began to see more clearly how the spirit of darkness is able to project itself into the material world. Whether it comes through music, books, television, the media, the words of family and friends, our dreams, or even our own thoughts, we need to be able to discern when something is coming from the realm of darkness.

As I continued to try to understand what I saw, I was brought back to a memory of when I was approximately nine years old that gave me insight in relation to the spirit of life I saw in my vision. One day I was riding my bicycle up a hill when I thought to myself, "Wouldn't it be great if this bicycle would go all by itself without my having to pedal it, and I could just sit back and enjoy the ride?" As I remembered this, I thought, "If the sealed, self-contained spirit of pure, white life that I saw lived inside of me, I would have a life force in me that would be my engine so I wouldn't have to push so hard. The life in me would do the work, create breakthrough, and go before me, and I could just sit back and enjoy the ride." I'm striving to live in this truth. I still have a long way to go to fully live in this reality, but a birthing has taken place in my life so that God has become my engine.

This principle of living by God's Spirit can be evident even within human relationships that are forged and created by the Holy Spirit. For example, I have a spiritual son in the faith, Pastor Joshua James Keinath, whom I have shepherded for about fifteen years. He is a musician, and we have such a spiritual connection that when he plays prophetic worship music as I am preaching or teaching, we don't need to have a plan to stay in unison as we minister together. In the spur of the moment the Holy Spirit will give him creative music to play, and at the same time the Spirit will lead me in proclaiming God's Word. We function together on the platform with such divine beauty and harmony. The fruit that comes from such times is greater than anything that would come from only playing memorized songs and preaching memorized sermons. Because we are both connected to the same Spirit, we function together with a precision and grace that could never be achieved by practice alone.

Learning to follow God's Spirit in this way takes sensitivity and surrender to the Holy Spirit inside of us. Once we allow God's Spirit to be our life force, we will enter into His power. Instead of constantly struggling on our own because we think it is all up to us—like I did as a child riding my bicycle up that steep hill—we will instead begin to trust God, knowing that He is working on our behalf, both in us and in our circumstances. Knowing that we don't have to control everything—that it doesn't all depend on us and that we can trust God—releases many burdens and produces rest. This is why Yeshua said:

> Come to Me, all who are weary and heavy-laden, and I will give you rest. Take My yoke upon you and learn from Me, for I am gentle and humble in heart, and you will find rest for your souls. For My yoke is easy and My burden is light.
>
> —MATTHEW 11:28–30

You may be asking yourself, "If Yeshua's yoke is easy and His burden is light, why is my life so hard?" Sometimes the reason is you're not letting Him be your life.

> He who has the Son has the life; he who does not have the Son of God does not have the life.
>
> —1 JOHN 5:12

Because of our reliance on trying to accomplish everything in our own flesh, we have a hard time receiving the revelation that our lives are in the Son. We don't know how to lay down our own initiatives and allow God to arise in us and be God. We think we have to do it all ourselves, so we end up tired and burned out.

God desires for us to completely trust and look to Him alone for all things. Once the Lord has stripped us of relying on ourselves and the world and has strengthened our faith to believe that He is going before us and supplying all our needs, we will enter into greater rest and peace.

I believe we can have the same peace the apostle John

(Yochanan) experienced while celebrating Passover with Yeshua. John simply leaned his head on Yeshua's bosom and rested. We can experience this same peace for our own lives when we learn to trust in God and stop relying on our flesh, others, and the world to supply all our needs.

Yeshua caused me to understand that the Spirit of life is within me and that I shouldn't look to the outside, where darkness dwells, for satisfaction or identity. Much of what lies outside ourselves is not of God but of the world. "For all that is in the world, the lust of the flesh and the lust of the eyes and the boastful pride of life, is not from the Father, but is from the world" (1 John 2:16).

As I've thought more of the vision over the years, I've come to believe that the pure, white, egg-shaped spirit of life that I saw is actually the deposit of the Holy Spirit that God imparts to us when we are born again. (See Romans 8:11; 2 Corinthians 1:22; and Ephesians 1:13.) His Spirit living within us is a reality!

It will take a lifetime for me to fully comprehend what I saw, but what I am sure of is this: knowing Jesus brings us into the life. Walking with God is not about behaving according to a certain moral code (even though behaving according to a moral code will emerge from it). It's about living from His light inside of you and resisting the darkness that surrounds us.

Many have mistaken being religious, with its many forms and rituals, with living by the life of the Spirit of God. Yeshua said, "It is the Spirit who gives life; the flesh profits nothing" (John 6:63). The Spirit that we have received is the same creative force that made the universe, the trees, the mountains, the sky, and all that is beautiful in this world. "In Him was life, and the life was the Light of men. The Light shines in the darkness, and the darkness did not comprehend it" (John 1:4–5). My goal is to be strengthened in God's Spirit and as a result walk in dominion over the powers of darkness, both for my own victory and to set others free.

9

PROGRAMMED?

OVER THE NEXT several months, I kept running after God. I was still living with my parents, going to church as often as I could, and trying to find work that felt meaningful. I began to feel as if there really wasn't anything left for me in Cleveland. I didn't have any friends, didn't have a career direction, and was butting heads with my family. I needed to make a fresh break. For the first time I got the idea that I wanted to start over in a completely new place, just God and me. So out of the blue I decided, "I'm going to move to California."

I planned to hitchhike. On the spur of the moment I packed a bag and headed on foot for the freeway, which was a couple of miles from our house. When I got to the freeway, it was close to midnight. I stuck out my thumb, and a guy picked me up almost immediately. As we drove, we got to talking. I pretty much told him my life story. Then when we were about an hour and a half down the road, he suddenly looked at me and said, "Listen, you really don't want to do this. This isn't what you should be doing with your life." After some talking, he convinced me that he was right. And with that, he turned us around and drove me back to Cleveland.

He'd already driven me an hour and a half down the road, so turning around meant it took him three hours to get back to where he was when he turned around. It still amazes me when I think back on this. God was protecting me. Looking back, sometimes I wonder if the man was an angel. Often when you hear hitchhikers' stories, something awful happens, but this guy was willing to go three hours out of his way to keep me from placing myself in harm's way. It was remarkable.

Now back home after my foiled plan to start over in California, I still kept talking about Jesus all the time, telling everybody about my vision of Him. And as it became apparent my "Jesus thing" wasn't going to go away on its own, my parents grew more alarmed. They decided to take things into their own hands and try to "save" me.

So one day out of the blue my dad told me, "Don't make any plans on Sunday. We're going to go talk to somebody about buying a restaurant. Maybe you and I will be in business together." I didn't think there was anything odd about his saying this. I was even hopeful that we might be in business together.

So Sunday came. I was up in my room, and my dad called me from the bottom of the stairs, saying it was time to go. I went downstairs, and my parents and I drove to a hotel on Chagrin Boulevard in Beachwood. Looking back, I feel like alarm bells should have been going off, that I should have known something was up, but I was completely unaware. Even when we went up to a regular hotel room rather than into a conference room, it didn't occur to me that something was odd.

When we arrived at the hotel room door, Dad knocked, and a short, middle-aged man opened it and invited us in. He had on a three-piece suit and seemed very distinguished. It was only when he shut the door that I realized there were two other men in the room—big guys, about six two and six one, respectively—standing back in the shadows. The more prominent man was in his fifties, and the two guys were probably in their mid- to late twenties. It was only then that things began to seem a little strange.

The leader introduced himself as Ted Patrick. You may recognize the name. Ted Patrick became famous in the 1970s and early 1980s as the leading cult deprogrammer in the United States. After he helped talk his son out of joining a cult, he hung up a shingle telling others he could save their kids as well. He was on national television talking about deprogramming and how cults brainwash people. You can still see some of these interviews on YouTube.[1]

Mr. Patrick invited me to sit down on one of the two beds in the room as my dad and mom watched. "Kirt, I want to talk to you about cults," he said.

"I'm not in a cult," I reacted.

"Then you've got nothing to worry about," he said. "I want to start by having you watch this film." One of the big guys flipped off the lights, and the other turned on a film projector. It was then I noticed that there was a screen already set up. They started showing me a film about Hare Krishnas. I didn't know what else to do but sit and watch.

At one point as the narrator talked, the film showed two little kids—maybe three or four years old—dressed up like the other Hare Krishnas playing together. "You see those kids?" Mr. Patrick said. "There's nothing I can do for them. Being in this cult is all they've known. They've spent their whole lives as Hare Krishnas. They've been programmed."

When the film ended, he took on a more authoritative air again. "Kirt," he said, "your parents tell me you've been living for twenty years like a normal person, and now suddenly you're seeing visions and chasing after Jesus. I consider it my personal challenge to snap you out of this. You've been giving all your money to the church and reading the Bible constantly. The Bible is the most dangerous book in the world. I am going to snap you out of this."

I stood up. "I'm not in a cult. I just believe that Jesus is the Messiah. Can I leave now?" I asked.

One of the big guys moved toward me and said, "Sit down."

"You're not going anywhere," the other said.

If I wasn't on high alert by all that had happened so far, I definitely was now.

"Well, can I use the bathroom then?"

Mr. Patrick gave me the nod that I could.

Alone in the bathroom I fell to my knees. I prayed, "Lord, I don't know where this is going. Please keep me through this."

When I came back out, they sat me down again, and Mr. Patrick and I debated whether I was programmed. He kept looking for some weakness in my argument. I told him I simply believed Jesus was the Messiah. No one had programmed me into believing it. The two goons kept watching quietly, making sure I didn't try to leave or get physical. It must have gone on an hour or so.

Next he explained that I was to go with one of his enforcers back to my parents' home. He slept in the other bed in my bedroom that night to ensure I didn't go anywhere. Looking back on this now, I am perplexed by how much I took all of this in stride.

"Pack some things, enough for a couple of weeks," he told me the next morning.

"Why?"

"We're going on a trip," he said.

When I'd packed, we went out to my van, and he got in the other side. There was no escape. He told me to start driving and he'd let me know where to turn as we needed to. We ended up driving all the way to San Diego, California, to where Ted Patrick lived and had his "rehabilitation house."

Ted Patrick's son lived there and ran the place. They confiscated my car keys and wallet, and I never left my room with more than the clothes on my back and the little spending money they gave me.

They would drop me off at the beach in the morning and then pick me up in the afternoon. Then after a few hours or so in my room, they'd take me to a bar, give me a little money, return my ID for the evening in case the bartender asked for it, and then leave me for the evening. They'd come back three or four hours later to get me.

We followed that routine for the two-and-a-half weeks I was there. But that was it. That was their deprogramming. Mr. Patrick's son and I hardly spoke to each other. I wasn't confronted or brought into any verbal arguments. I didn't have to watch any more films. Maybe the idea was to get me away from whoever they thought was programming me so I could clear my head and snap out of it. Or maybe after a while they saw I wasn't as crazy and abnormal as my parents had led them to believe. I don't know. I just stayed with his son in his rehabilitation house. I didn't see Mr. Patrick again until the end.

When I saw him that time, I asked again, "Can I go home?"

He just said, "Yeah, OK. You can go home."

When they gave me back my keys and my wallet, I went straight to my van and got out of there as quickly as I could. (Some of the people who went through his deprogramming pushed back and accused him of kidnapping. He eventually went to jail for it. It never even occurred to me to report him to the police. I just wanted to get out of there.)

In actuality I felt very bad for my parents about all of this. I knew they must have paid a good deal of money to have me deprogrammed, and I felt like they got swindled. I also realized, probably for the first time, just how much my following Jesus upset them.

I knew, though, that I couldn't turn back. I had decided to follow Jesus. I did realize, however, that it might be a good idea to be a little less vocal about my faith for a while with my family. While I was living under my parents' roof, I could at least do that much.

At the end of the day, going through the deprogramming didn't make anything better with my family. We never talked about what had happened, but there was always a tension in the air. One night the five of us were sitting around the dinner table—my mom; my dad; my brother, Mitchell; my sister, Susie; and me—and all of a sudden Mitchell jumped up from his chair and stormed at me in an angry outburst. I think he was just so frustrated and shaken that he didn't know what to do. I was no longer the brother he knew—something had taken me over.

The feeling of not knowing who I was anymore was similar with my Jewish friends, though nothing ever came to fists. Most of them simply distanced themselves from me. The best I got from any of them was when one of them with whom I'd shared my vision said, "Well, I can tell you're sincere." But it was still a disconnect for him. The road I was walking was weird, foreign, and distasteful, and they didn't want any part of it. Believing in Jesus carried such a stigma, and my Jewish friends and community found it easiest to simply avoid me. It was a difficult time.

But it would get worse before it got better.

One of the craziest things that happened was at a Jewish wedding where a girl I had never met came over and initiated a relationship with me. We started dating, and after we had been dating a few months, word got back to me that this girl wasn't dating me because she liked me but to convert me back to Judaism. It turned out she wanted to become some kind of hero to the Jewish community by saving me from believing in Jesus.

When I learned this was what she was doing, I told her, "You don't know who you're messing with. You're messing with the wrong person." Then I broke up with her. I thought that would be the end of it.

She lived in a home with three other girls, though, and I thought one of these other girls was very cute. So about three weeks after I'd broken up with the first girl, I went over to the house and asked to see this other girl. One of the roommates went to get her while I waited in their front room.

While standing there looking out the front room's window, I suddenly heard this *"Bam! Bam! Bam!"* coming down the hallway from where the girls' bedrooms were. Jolted, I quickly turned and faced this big, solid guy who was about six two now standing less than a foot from me. He had a knife, and before I could react, he stuck it into my chest. Then he knocked me on the ground, and as I was sitting there, he started kicking me in the face with his big hiking boots.

After about thirty seconds he stopped kicking me, and I was able to make my way out the door and drive myself to the hospital, though just barely. I arrived in shock, and the doctors found blood in the bottom of my lung, so they drained it and kept me overnight.

The police came soon after I was put into a room. After getting my story, they went and arrested the guy for felonious assault. I testified at his arraignment, but wanting to follow Jesus' words about turning the other cheek, I said I didn't want to involve myself in pressing charges.

I was told that the man who'd attacked me was part of an extremist Jewish group called the Jewish Defense League (JDL). The JDL is a group that uses violence against anti-Semitism and those they feel are a threat to the Jewish community. I'm not sure why he attacked me. If it was because he was just mentally unbalanced or if somehow I was a target due to his ideology, I don't know. What I do know is that many Orthodox Jews consider Jews who believe in Jesus to be a danger to the Jewish people. For them, becoming a believer in Yeshua and trying to convince other Jews to believe in Him is like spiritually killing the Jewish people, just as Hitler physically killed Jews during the Holocaust. This is because they believe that worshipping God through Yeshua is idolatry.

I'm not sure what happened to my attacker. Praise God that all I have to show for this violent stabbing is a scar on my chest that is still there to this day. Everything else healed without complication.

Little did I know, my next challenge was going to be a lot more psychological.

10

MASHUGANA FOR JESUS

Y PARENTS STILL didn't know what to do with me. They had sold their house and moved into an apartment. One day they asked a Jewish psychiatrist to come to the apartment to examine me. He was a very frail-looking man, not at all imposing—short, somewhat red-faced, balding, and red-haired. When my parents asked me to talk with him, I wasn't shaken by it. Maybe it would appease some of their concerns that something was wrong with me. I wasn't scared of this guy.

But maybe I should have been.

He was friendly and unassuming. He asked me about what was going on in my life. I saw it as a chance to share my testimony, so I told him everything. I told him how lost I'd felt when my high school wrestling career ended short of my dreams and about my experimenting with new age mysticism and how God intervened by giving me a vision of Jesus on the cross. He listened, so I went into further detail. I told him I didn't know what would have happened to me if I hadn't met Jesus and that accepting Him as my Messiah saved my life.

The interview lasted about an hour. When it was over, he gently said goodbye to my parents and me and left. I figured that was that.

Later that day, when I was with some Christian friends (I had Christian friends by this time), I told them about the experience. I actually said, "I made mincemeat out of that psychiatrist." I was in for a wake-up call!

About a week later, when I returned to my parents' apartment after work, there were two suitcases sitting in front of the door, and my mom and dad were obviously waiting for me. My dad pointed out the window of our apartment to the main parking lot for the complex. "You see that police car down there?" he said. "They're waiting for us. You can come with us in our car, or they're going to come and take you. You've been probated to the psychiatric ward of Mount Sinai Hospital" (which was in Cleveland).

I'd fallen for the psychiatrist's trap hook, line, and sinker. He wasn't there to hear my testimony but to get enough condemning information to have me probated! To him, my vision of Jesus was proof that I was having hallucinations and was a danger to myself and other people. My sense that God was calling me to something special meant I had delusions of grandeur. I was pretty young and naive, but it didn't take me long to understand that I had been set up!

This turned into one of the most difficult experiences of my life. Once I was admitted to the psychiatric floor at the hospital, there was no way of escape. I was completely a prisoner, with much less freedom than I'd had with Ted Patrick in California. I was a young, energetic guy, and suddenly I was confined to a very small space. I had no outlet for my energies. If I sat too long, my legs would start bouncing with energy. I was required to go to group therapy—roughly twenty people sitting in a circle talking about what had brought them there. Still young in the faith, I was armed with truth but often lacked in compassion. In the group setting a woman said she hoped her husband, who had recently passed away, was in heaven.

"Did your husband believe in Jesus?" I asked.

"Well, no. We're Jewish."

"Then he's not in heaven," I said.

You can imagine how that went over!

After that the decision was made that I should be medicated. When they offered the pills, they told me, "You can either take these, or we'll strap you down and inject them." I took the pills, and they made me feel worse. I felt this stressful energy in my body and a bit sedated at the same time. I had no sane, friendly person to talk to because I was surrounded by mental patients. It was scary and depressing. The most vivid and saddest scene I remember is one of a young woman who looked to be in her twenties. She was medium to tall, her dark hair totally disheveled, and she walked around with her shoulders slumped over and her head held down. She looked extremely depressed and tormented and to me appeared suicidal. It is a very dark and haunting memory.

Meanwhile, at that time, it was possible for the State of Ohio to hold me in the ward for two months on the word of a psychiatrist. After that, there would be a board review to determine if I needed to be detained there longer. I felt as if my every action was scrutinized and evaluated. It was boredom, anxiety, and monotony, doing the same thing day after day under the stupor of drugs, with watchful, critical eyes everywhere. The only reprieve was the art therapy class that was at least a bit of a distraction, but it happened only once a week.

My parents came to visit several times, which I think was a bad idea. They were possibly even less comfortable with the confines of the psychiatric floor than I was. I think it disgusted my dad to have his oldest son in such a place—even though it could be argued that he was the one responsible for my being there. There were people all over wandering around like zombies, totally drugged out, and I was among them.

I persevered, clung to God, and prayed that Jesus would keep me through it all and that I'd get out as soon as possible.

After being in the psychiatric ward of Mount Sinai Hospital for two months, a board review determined whether I could be released. The board consisted not just of the psychiatrist who filled out the paperwork that got the patient hospitalized but also of a number of independent psychiatrists. During the review, which felt like a trial, I presented my case and answered their questions, and they decided I could be released.

After being discharged, I had to go back to the psychiatrist who had probated me because I agreed to some outpatient follow up. After a few sessions I remember telling him, "I don't really feel like these sessions are doing me any good. You're not helping me."

Rather than listening, he started attacking me. "You are very sick," he said. "That's why you're here. Your mind is very, very sick." I ended up discontinuing my sessions with him, getting off his prescriptions, and stopping all psychiatric care. By the grace of God here I am now, forty years later, never having taken a psychiatric drug or seen a psychiatrist since—and I am being used of the Lord all over the world.

At the end of the day, the Lord used this experience to root me in Him. I remember one day walking around in the hallway of the psychiatric unit. I was feeling really alone, not knowing where this all was going to land or when I was going to get out. All of a sudden in my mind's eye I saw Jesus high above in the heavens, and somehow I sensed that I was in Him and He was in me. I knew He was triumphant high above the earth and I was victorious in Him. I knew in that instant I had a future and a destiny in my Messiah.

Oftentimes God's light shines into our lives the brightest when we are in the darkest places.

Once out of the hospital it took me a few months to feel like myself again. I still had all of this pent-up energy in my body from being trapped in that ward, and I couldn't stop bobbing my leg up and down whenever I sat for an extended time. Slowly my system calmed down.

I continued to reach out to God and found a Messianic synagogue called Tikvat Yisrael that I started attending. I met a girl there, and we started dating. As it turned out, she was bouncing back and forth between Tikvat Yisrael and a Hasidic group called Chabad-Lubavitch, which is a very Orthodox Jewish sect. Chabad-Lubavitch was run by a rebbe, which is sort of a mix between a rabbi, spiritual leader, and community patriarch. The Chabad-Lubavitch rebbe, the late Menachem Schneerson, has been perhaps the most influential Orthodox Jew in the last several hundred years. His talks were being simulcast all over the world, and groups and congregations would gather locally to hear these broadcasts. I went with her to one of these simulcasts.

The room they met in was sort of an L shape. As you came in, you were met by a table with some refreshments, and then you went around the corner to see the screen of the simulcast. It was at this meeting that the Spirit of God again marked me. As I was standing by the refreshment table, out of nowhere I was filled with a red light. In the light I saw the word Jew. It was like being filled with a thick ray of light from heaven. Once again the experience lasted only a second. As quickly as it came, it was gone. I had no idea what it meant at the time, though over the years, I've come to the conclusion it was God divinely affirming that I was still Jewish to prepare me for what lay ahead.

You see, since 1978, when I received Yeshua as my Messiah, I have had to stand against my own people treating me as if I was no longer Jewish. In reality this makes no logical sense. Many in Chabad-Lubavitch believe their rebbe, Menachem Schneerson, is the Messiah, even though he has passed away. Many other Orthodox Hasidic Jews from different Jewish sects pray at their dead rebbe's grave, thinking he will take their petitions to God or even answer them himself. So the truth is they relate to their rebbes the same way I relate to Yeshua.

The prejudice of the Pharisees who rejected Jesus in the New Testament has been passed on to every succeeding generation of Jewish people. Yeshua said in John 16:2 that Jewish believers in Him would be banned from the synagogues and that the leaders of the synagogue would think they were doing service to God by excommunicating us. Hear what John says happened after Messiah Jesus healed a blind man.

> The Jews then did not believe it of him, that he had been blind and had received sight, until they called the parents of the very one who had received his sight, and questioned them, saying, "Is this your son, who you say was born blind? Then how does he now see?" His parents answered them and said, "We know that this is our son, and that he was born blind; but how he now sees, we do not know; or who opened his eyes, we do not know. Ask him; he is of age, he will speak for himself." His parents said this because they were afraid of the Jews; for the Jews had already agreed that if anyone confessed

Him to be Christ, he was to be *put out of the synagogue.* For this reason his parents said, "He is of age; ask him."

—JOHN 9:18–23, EMPHASIS ADDED

Jews today reject any Jew who believes in Jesus, not for logical reasons but because it has been passed down to them by osmosis, going all the way back to the Pharisees who called for Jesus' crucifixion. So knowing all the resistance I would face from the Jewish community, Father God strengthened me and affirmed me in my Jewishness at that Orthodox gathering by filling me with His Spirit in the form of a beam of red light that went through me with the word Jew inside it.

I know this sounds out of the box, but God is not limited in how He chooses to manifest Himself, whether it be in the form of the rainbow-colored light that Ezekiel saw (Ezekiel 1:28), the dove that John the Baptist saw (Matthew 3:16), or the tongues of fire that appeared over the disciples' heads on the day of Pentecost (Acts 2:3).

11

G. J. KIRT

A s I sought Him more, God started dealing with me about some of the issues that were getting between us. One of the first was my smoking. Every time I felt I needed something to calm or settle me, I would, without thinking about it, reach for a cigarette. I had been deceived into thinking I would receive life and satisfaction in the smokes. I was looking to death for life. It is interesting that many times I can literally see a spirit of death on people who have smoked their whole lives. I can often look at people and tell that they have been smokers for the past forty years because of the pale of death that is on their faces. The spirit of death is actually visible. *Baruch HaShem* (Praise God!)—God delivered me of my smoking addiction.

I also got rid of all my pornography. Not only did I realize that pornography hindered my walk with God, but by engaging with it, I was opening the door to spiritual darkness and evil. I comprehended that if I continued to yield to this temptation, I would not be protected by God's light but would instead put myself in a spiritual realm where Satan could attack me.

As I was in this season of repentance, turning away from cigarettes and pornography, I was sitting in a chair one morning having a cup of tea and reaching out to God. I wasn't expecting anything to happen when all of a sudden the living Spirit of God literally appeared above my head. It was similar to an Acts chapter 2 experience, when the Spirit of the Lord appeared above the disciples' heads as a flame of fire. It wasn't a thought or a picture in my mind. The Spirit of God actually appeared above my head, twirling around in all the colors of a rainbow.

Then all of a sudden He came through my head and took possession of my inner self. He spoke four simple words, "I am a servant," in and through me. I heard His voice as clearly as I can hear my own voice right now. But I didn't hear it through my ears, although the sound was as solid and precise as if it was through my ears. I can't explain how I heard His voice; I just did. Then as quickly as the encounter started, it was over, just like that.

This experience was not some vague feeling or mental impression; rather, the power of God came upon me suddenly. I could not have helped the experience along nor could I have stopped it from happening. I've been praying since 1981 to better understand this heavenly encounter and receive a deeper revelation of the words He spoke to me: "I am a servant."

Afterward, if I wasn't already sold out to God (which I thought I was), I knew I absolutely had to give my life over to Him completely. I was done with everything else in life. I wanted a way to live completely and solely for God—no turning back.

I thought, "Lord, how can I give everything over to You? How can I live totally for You alone?" I got a hold of a magazine article that described different Christian communities and monasteries around the world. I decided a Christian community wouldn't suffice because there would be women there and I might get distracted from focusing on God alone, so I opted for a monastery where there would be only men. One of the monasteries this article reviewed was called St. Augustine's House in Michigan. I called. A monk picked up the phone.

I said, "I want to join and become a monk."

After a pause he responded, "Well, it doesn't work like that. First you need to come down and visit for a week or so. Then you go back home, pray about it, and come back for a second visit. Then you do the same thing again, and if after your third visit you're still feeling this way, we can talk about you being here long term."

"No," I said. "I don't need to do that. I'm coming down, and I'm going to join. I want to become a monk."

He tried to caution me again, but he saw it was no good, so we set up a time for me to visit.

When I left Cleveland to become a monk, I was sure that was it. I said goodbye to my parents. I said goodbye to the Jewish girl I'd been dating and attending the Messianic synagogue with. This was it. They would never see me again—at least not without my habit (the garment worn by monks). My family went to a restaurant for our final meal together. My parents probably felt like this was one of the saddest days in their lives, their Jewish son going off to become a monk. It was the last straw. I remember the cloud of darkness that hung over us all as we ate.

The next day a friend of mine drove me to the monastery.

Three days later he got a call. I was crying. "Would you come get me?" I was in anguish. It was not what this Jewish boy had envisioned. It was too strict, too ritualistic, too formal. There was hardly any talk. The only positive memory I have is that they would play B. J. Thomas' Christian albums at dinner. It was not that this place wasn't right for the monks; it just wasn't a good fit for me. I wanted to get out of there—and fast!

When I got home, I spent a day in my room, refusing to come out. I was humiliated. I felt like such a failure and completely defeated. Here I had just told my family and friends that I was leaving for good and that they were not going to see me again (at least as the Kirt they knew), and three days later I was back home, literally crying in my bed.

Shortly after, my parents asked me to move out. They hadn't expected me back. They couldn't take it anymore and frankly just didn't know what to do with me. I was erratic and still very vocal about my faith. Somehow they found and reached out to a Messianic rabbi in Cleveland who agreed to take me into his house. I was with him for a couple of months.

The feeling that there really wasn't anything for me in Cleveland anymore was stronger than ever. I wanted to move someplace new and start over with just me and Jesus. The scale tipped in this direction completely on a very hot summer day.

It was about ninety degrees and sunny. I was working for an electrician, and we were wiring a home. My boss told me to go up into the attic and connect some wiring. With it being as hot as it was, I'd worn a tank top to work, and when I went up into the attic, the fiberglass insulation started sticking all over my sweaty skin. It must have been at least 120 degrees up there. When I got the job done, I was so glad to come back down to where it was only ninety again, and all I wanted was to get home, take a shower, and wash off the insulation that was itching, burning, and otherwise causing significant skin irritation. But that was not to be.

"Did you double-check all your connections?" my boss asked me. "I don't want any uncovered connections up there."

"Everything's good," I assured him.

He looked at me. "Are you sure?"

"Yes," I said. "I'm very sure."

He thought for a moment. "Why don't you just go back up and double-check, just to make sure."

I got obstinate. "I'm not going back up there. It's 120 degrees up there, and the fiberglass insulation is already all over me!"

On this day, he wasn't a patient man, so he got obstinate back. "You go up there and double-check the wiring, or I'll fire you!"

"I'm not going back up there!" I said.

To which he replied, "You're fired."

I walked off the jobsite. That was the end of my employment with him.

I went back to my apartment, showered, and decided that was it. It was time to put Cleveland in the rearview mirror. It was just going to be me and Jesus from here on out. I remembered a guy I met standing outside a Christian coffeehouse a few years earlier. I said to him, "What's your name?"

He said, "G. J. Eddy."

"'G. J. Eddy?'" I replied with a questioning look.

"Yeah," he shot back. "God, Jesus, and Eddy."

In that moment, I identified with G. J. Eddy. I was going to launch out with just God and Jesus. G. J. Kirt.

I got out a map of the United States that I had and laid it out on the floor of the apartment. I said, "Lord, I want to start over with just You and me. I want to build a life with just You and me." I took a coin, flipped it into the air, and let it fall on the map. It landed on a place called Park Rapids, Minnesota. I took that as a sign from the Lord, so that's where I was going to go.

At the time, I owned an old, orange AMC Gremlin. I loaded it up with what I needed, which wasn't much, and headed out on my big adventure. There I was, just me and Jesus, starting from scratch on the way to my own personal promised land.

Driving from Cleveland to Minnesota, I daydreamed about maybe starting a church there, but as it turned out, there's not much in Park Rapids, Minnesota. It appeared to be part of a Native American reservation. I remember going into a restaurant and finding it basically empty. I sat down, and at a table across from me was a Native American girl who just stared at me. This Jewish boy was in a very foreign environment.

It was not a promising start.

I wandered around in search of a job, but the only potential employer I found was a ski club just out of town. They weren't going to be hiring for two months because the snow had not yet fallen. Additionally, to get the job, I would have had to buy a bunch of ski equipment, which I didn't have money for and, oh yeah, learn how to ski. I determined pretty quickly that if I stayed in Park Rapids, Minnesota, I was going to freeze to death if I didn't starve to death first.

I needed a new plan.

Thinking about freezing to death made me realize that I needed to go somewhere warm so that when winter came, I would be able to survive. I counted my money and determined that if I drove pretty much straight south, I could get to Corpus Christi, Texas. My logic was, "It's next to the ocean, and it has a beach, so it must be warm." I had been on vacations with my parents to Florida and California, which were both on the ocean, and it was warm there. So I just figured Corpus Christi must be warm too, since it's also on the ocean. (Like I said, I was a late bloomer.) I packed my things and headed south.

I stopped to eat along the way at a Sambo's Restaurant in Kansas City, Missouri, but when I finished and went back out to my car, it wouldn't start. I didn't have enough money to both get my car fixed and get to Corpus Christi, so I was stranded.

There were many restaurants along this stretch of road where Sambo's was, so I just crossed the street and started walking. I went into the first restaurant I came to and asked if they were hiring. They were. The manager gave me an application. For my address I wrote that I was living out of my car in the Sambo's Restaurant parking lot across the street.

After I finished the application, leaving the phone number space blank, I called the manager over to explain. "My car broke down," I said, "on the way to Corpus Christi. I do not presently have a phone. I'm available and ready to start."

As you may imagine, he didn't ask me to come back for a second interview. I very quickly realized I was not going to get a job with no place to live other than my car and no phone number.

I went back to the Sambo's Restaurant and went into the bathroom. I said in my heart to the Lord, "Father, I'm going all the way. I'm going to trust and rely on You alone completely."

After taking all the money I had out of my wallet, I threw my wallet and all that was in it into the bathroom's wastebasket. Next I took off my glasses, which I'd needed since the third grade, and threw them in the wastebasket. My eyes were so bad—like -10 in one eye and -11 in the other—that without them I could not see a person's eyes from six feet away. Faces looked like one big blur of color to me. But I was trusting God for everything: my finances, the healing of my vision, everything. It was God, Jesus, and Kirt—that's it.

Next I went to the waitress who had served me and gave her the remaining money—it was all I had to my name. Then I took the keys to my AMC Gremlin out of my pocket and told her the vehicle was in the parking lot and the car was hers.

When you're down, you can either quit or go all in. I went all in. (I wouldn't advise anyone else to do these things. I'm just recalling—with a good deal of head shaking—what I did.) Not being limited by the need for gas money anymore, my options were now wide open. I decided to hitchhike to the deep forest of California, where I would fast for forty days and forty nights like Jesus did.

Nobody picked me up the first day, and I spent that first night sleeping in the weeds on the side of the road. The following day the same thing happened; no one picked me up. I ended up sleeping that night on a fiberglass bench in the bowling alley section of a 24/7 sports complex.

The third day in the late morning a Camaro pulled over and picked me up. The guy told me he was heading to Amarillo. He seemed friendly, and as we got to talking, he said he had an old friend who had been a neighbor in Florida and now had a Tex-Mex restaurant in Amarillo. He was driving to see him. If I wanted, he told me, I could go with him and he'd get me a job working in the restaurant. Although I had intended to go to California, I thought maybe this was God's leading, so I agreed to go with him.

As we continued driving, he told me he was going to start an import/export company and asked me if I knew anything about it. "Maybe we could be in business together?" he mused. He bought me lunch and seemed like a good guy.

When we arrived in Amarillo, we spent the first night at his friend's condominium and the next day got rooms at the local YMCA because they were the cheapest accommodations. As he'd promised, his friend gave me a job in his Tex-Mex restaurant and fronted me some money, and I went to work right away as a line cook.

After a few weeks I was sitting in my room one day, waiting to go to work, when I heard heavy boots coming up the stairs and then running down the hall past my room—*boom, boom, boom, boom!* I looked out my door to see a mob of FBI agents in their blue jackets storming down the hallway. Who were they after? The guy who had given me a ride! It turned out he was wanted for armed robbery in Florida, and it became a federal offense when he crossed state lines. They hauled him away in handcuffs, and I never saw him again.

In the meantime things weren't going well at the restaurant. The problem was that since I had thrown my glasses away, I had to get right up against the orders to be able to read them. This was an issue because my place in the line was about eight feet from where the orders hung. So I was constantly leaving my place to go butt my head between other cooks to get close enough to read the orders. This was not appreciated.

So after two months I took the money I had saved and bought a bus ticket to where my aunt lived in Los Angeles. I called her in advance, and once I told her all that had happened, she seemed happy to let me stay until I got settled. I got a job as a graveyard-shift dishwasher at a twenty-four-hour restaurant. I remember riding my little cousin's bicycle to and from work, thinking to myself, "Man, oh man, Lord. I trusted You to make me something, and this is where I am? If I ever live to make $100,000 a year, it'll be a miracle."

It wasn't that I cared about the money. It was just that I felt I was going nowhere fast. My brother was in law school, and my sister was doing well in college, and here I was on the other side of the country, waking up in the middle of the night and riding my little cousin's bicycle to work, where I was washing dishes. There's nothing wrong with washing dishes; I just saw no future in it for myself. I had no idea where my life was going.

Thankfully, Someone did.

12

CYNTHIA

I'D BEEN IN California staying with my aunt for several months when my dad called and asked me to come home. I was a little skeptical after all the disagreements we'd had, but it felt as if he was implying, "You're still my son. You belong with your family." So I flew home.

Unfortunately we still didn't get along. We were just in two different places.

I hadn't been back in Cleveland much more than a month when I saw a familiar face while I was out in Pepper Pike one night at a local bar called the Lion and Lamb (the same bar and grill I was in the night I met Jesus). Her name was Cynthia. Not only had we gone to Orange High School together, but she had lived only one door away from us in Pepper Pike when my parents had the big house with the pool. We were even at the same bus stop every morning to go to school. I had a vague memory of her, but because the houses on the street were fairly far apart and because we ran in different circles, I didn't really know her, and we'd never talked much before.

But running into her created another witnessing opportunity, so at the Lion and Lamb that night, I started telling her about my vision and my faith in Jesus. She sat quietly, eyes wide, listening intently. I had no idea at the time that what I was saying was affecting her deep down in her spirit.

Cynthia was raised considerably differently than I was—her family was very conservative and attended church regularly. She went to Michigan State University when she left Cleveland, and despite the sincerity of her faith, she began to question what she had been taught to believe. As she began meeting all these people who came from different backgrounds and cultures and had different faiths—Muslims, Hindus, and so on—she began to wonder, "How can I be sure that what I have been taught is the truth? They all seem like good, sincere people. I mean, these people grew up with different backgrounds or in different countries where they were taught a different religion than me. Who's to say that I am right and they are not? If I grew up in their country or came from their background, I would probably believe what they believe. They're convinced that what they believe is right. They seem more religious than most of the people I know. So how do I know if the Jesus I was taught to believe in really is the way to God? How do I know if they're not the ones who are right and I'm wrong?" She started attending a Bible study around that time, and when every book they studied was by the same guy, she started thinking it was a cult. That added to her doubt, disillusionment, and sense of being spiritually lost.

So despite her drifting, she began earnestly praying that God would reveal Himself to her and show her if she was right to put her faith in Jesus. She told God she could not believe in Jesus until He showed her that Jesus really was the way. Alongside that she made another request that she didn't share with me until much later. She asked that God would bring a man who knew Him into her life for her to marry. She also requested, if it wasn't too much trouble, that he be cute. (Thankfully she felt I answered both those prayers!) While she was waiting on God to answer those two prayers, her spiritual foundations eroded and she drifted from what she had been taught growing up.

As I shared my testimony of Jesus with her, she said it was like a lightning bolt struck and sent electricity through her body. God spoke to her right there in that bar, saying, "I am the way, the truth, and the life." The Spirit of God arrested her. I didn't realize what was going on or that God was using me, her Jewish neighbor growing up, to bring her to Himself. It most definitely was not one-sided, though. Although Cynthia had gotten lost spiritually while in college, she nevertheless had something that I needed. She was grounded in a way that I was not.

Part of this, I think, can be attributed to her upbringing. Her parents were very practical and moral people. But beyond that I think it is just God's gifting, favor, and grace on her. She is able to look at circumstances and relationships objectively so she doesn't react to things personally. If somebody does or says something that would potentially offend or cause hurt feelings, Cynthia will usually be able to perceive the root of that person's behavior and not be hurt. This is just one of many examples of how Jesus continues to use my bride to help keep me grounded. She is full of goodness and is strong in so many areas where I am weak. I'm pretty sure, despite my faith, that my life would have been shipwrecked had it not been for my meeting Cynthia.

We started dating. Cynthia's parents couldn't figure me out. They could see on the one hand how passionate I was for God and how well I knew the Bible. (I had memorized a lot of Scripture.) On the other hand, because I was not on a successful career path and because of the way I looked, they were afraid. When I picked Cynthia up for our first date, I was holding a beer bottle and wearing a cowboy hat, a homemade rope belt, and a black cowboy shirt. Her mom answered the door, took one look at me, and went to discuss with Cynthia the wisdom of her going out with me. She was concerned, to say the least.

I'm sure to her parents' chagrin, we began seeing each other almost every night of the week. Less than three months into this, we were window-shopping one day and saw a ring she liked for $28. It was a small, fourteen-carat gold ring with a cross that had a diamond chip in its center. Off the cuff I asked, "If I bought you that ring, would you marry me?"

She looked me in the eye to see if I was serious. When she saw I was, she smiled and said, "Yes, I'll marry you."

It was unplanned, but God assured me it was the right decision. Shortly after I proposed, I was lying down one afternoon, looking out the window and thinking of Cynthia. All of a sudden in my mind's eye I saw a road in front of me, and at the end of it was Cynthia with a rainbow over her. I felt like the Lord was saying, "Cynthia is the right path for you, and My promise and blessing is over this marriage."

About two months before we got married, I had another dream that has marked me significantly over the years. I found myself in a rectangular room, maybe forty feet long by twenty-five feet wide. It was dark. There was a window on one wall and another window on the opposite wall. All of a sudden through one window all the colors of a rainbow streamed into the room. The light had substance, like a thick, three-dimensional crepe-paper streamer you'd string across the room for a birthday party. It was alive, moving, and flowing like a spiritual river. It appeared to be about a foot and a half from top to bottom and streamed deeply into room. I knew it was the same Spirit that several years before had appeared above my head, filled me, and then spoken the words "I am a servant" into my inner man, as I described earlier in this book. I started walking toward it, knowing it was God.

I then followed the Spirit of life to the window it had entered the room through and stuck my head out to see what was there. All I saw was color, an eternity of color. It was like when you look up at the sky on a cloudless day and see only blue, except the color was not just in the sky—everywhere was color. Again I knew it was the Spirit of God, and I called out to Him, "Come and live inside me." Then I clearly heard from deep within me, from what felt like my interior stomach area, the word *eternity*. Immediately after I heard the word *eternity*, the dream shifted.

I was now looking out the window on the opposite side of the room. There I saw chaos. If you've ever seen the movie *The Wizard of Oz*, you may recall that when the cyclone came, Dorothy looked out the window, and all she saw was things randomly swirling in the wind. What I saw was like that—randomness and chaos.

Then suddenly the dream shifted for the last time. In the last phase I was walking down a street and I was very calm, not thinking about anything. I came to an intersection, and there was a car there that had been in some kind of a wreck. As I approached, I saw that there was a man, and he was lying half inside and half outside of the car. His body was in one piece, but his legs and midsection were still in the car, and the rest of him was on the street. He had burns all over from the car wreck. I also saw that he was dark-skinned—at the time I thought he was African American.

Without any thought I stuck my hand out toward him, and

the colors that I had asked to come and live inside me earlier in the dream flowed out of my fingertips toward the man. As the colors touched him, they healed him. Then the dream ended.

I wondered at the dream and felt it meant I had a calling to minister healing to African American people, but I didn't immediately pursue anything more with it at the time. It did bolster my faith and expectation in the supernatural, but I wasn't sure what to do. (By the way, as you may know, I now minister to hundreds of thousands in Africa—but more about that later.)

That was the fall of 1982, shortly before Cynthia and I got married on January 15, 1983.

Even before we were engaged, Cynthia and I had started informally talking about our possible future together. We went to a library one day and began researching Bible colleges. I also started making some phone calls for Bible school recommendations, and someone suggested Toccoa Falls Bible College in northeast Georgia. It had a reputation as a solid, Bible-believing school, and Cynthia liked the idea of being near the Appalachian and Blue Ridge Mountains of Georgia. Although it was officially listed as a nondenominational school, it was affiliated with the Christian and Missionary Alliance (CMA), which I was not familiar with at the time. I applied and got in. The night of our wedding we drove out of Cleveland and headed for Toccoa Falls. We got married on a Saturday evening and started attending classes on Monday.

I'm pretty sure my life would have been shipwrecked had I not met Cynthia. We got married on January 15, 1983, and God has used Cynthia to help keep me grounded.

I think the wedding was really hard for my parents. Most Jewish weddings are very robust and celebratory, with a party-like atmosphere. Ours matched my in-laws more—very prim and proper—and took place in Cynthia's parents' country club, where not many Jews were members. I think the atmosphere just added to the distance my parents felt toward me. On top of that, I was not marrying a Jewish girl, and I was heading out to a Christian college to become a pastor. (By the way it was not so much that I wanted to be a pastor; it was just that I wanted to spend all my time seeking God and studying the Bible, and being a pastor would allow me to do that.)

Cynthia's dad reluctantly let his daughter marry me; he wasn't too sure about me. He was an engineer and saw the world very matter-of-factly. He was very practical and business oriented. Of course Cynthia was an adult and could make her own decision. But when the minister asked, "Who gives this bride to the groom in marriage?" He said, "Ginnie," referring to Cynthia's mom. I don't know if he just couldn't bring himself to do it, was nervous and misspoke, or said, "Ginnie and I," and we just didn't hear correctly. All I know is that at the time, he felt releasing his daughter to me was a big risk and a step into the unknown.

Without our knowledge, before we got married, Cynthia's dad and mom had actually flown from Cleveland to Atlanta and then drove to Toccoa Falls Bible College to check it out when they heard I was planning on attending. Her dad met with the president of the school and must have been satisfied, because I didn't find out about it until after I graduated.

In the years to come, though, Cynthia's father and I became close. Cynthia's parents eventually became real believers in us and our ministry, and her dad came to truly respect and appreciate me. One memory that really touches me is that all the way up until Cynthia's dad passed away, in his nineties, he tried to never miss watching (and in his later years just hearing due to his vision problems) *Discovering the Jewish Jesus* on television. This meant a lot to me since my own parents could not relate to my faith or my ministry. At that time, my dad had never commented that he had seen my television program. It also was very meaningful to have my father-in-law's support, because I had a lot of respect for him. He was very humble and successful. Cynthia's parents both were huge blessings to me and our family over the years.

When I graduated from Toccoa Falls Bible College, I was planning to become a pastor. I had no idea where God would take me in ministry.

When I was a pastor in Reynoldsville, Pennsylvania, I led my first outdoor evangelistic meeting, which was a citywide festival.

It is always a rich experience to film *Discovering the Jewish Jesus* from Jerusalem.

Although Israel can be hostile to Jewish believers in Yeshua, God has opened doors for me there to share the good news. Here, I am sharing Yeshua with Holocaust survivors in the Old City of Jerusalem.

In a park in Kyiv, Ukraine, Cynthia and I had an opportunity to preach the good news of Messiah Yeshua to Jewish people who didn't know Him.

By some estimates, the crowd at our crusade in Gulu, Uganda, reached fifty thousand, though some believe it was higher. Whatever the number, we know that city was profoundly touched by the power of God and people were healed and set free.

When we enter cities in Africa to host crusades, people line the streets to welcome us. In nation after nation, we've seen an incredible hunger for the gospel and God's supernatural power.

We have seen incredible demonstrations of God's power around the world. In one nation we visited, a demonized woman was dramatically delivered. You can see the difference in her countenance in these pictures. The total horror visible on her face (right) disappeared and was replaced with God's peace and joy (middle picture).

This woman was unable to walk without her crutches and was healed during one of our crusades in Africa.

Here, I am speaking at a pastors' conference in Abakaliki, Nigeria. We consider it an important part of our ministry to help equip pastors and to strengthen them. Whenever we go to Africa, we create opportunities to train pastors and encourage them in their walk with God and in their callings as ministers of the gospel.

In Brazil a woman thanks me after being delivered of a demon.

Milla Rose was totally blind and used to just sit and beg at the hotel each day. But when I commanded, "Blind eyes, be opened," at our crusade in Lira, Uganda, she was miraculously healed. Two years later (below), she was still able to see, and those who know her say she's happy all the time.

Cynthia is my partner in life and in ministry. Here, we are ministering together in Africa (above) and on the set of *Discovering the Jewish Jesus* (below).

During a visit to Malawi, I was able to pray with Lazarus Chakwera, who later became president of the nation.

We held a crusade in Kakuma, Kenya, where one of the largest refugee camps in the world is located. Here, I am with members of the Turkana people group, who are indigenous to this area.

In 2017 I was able to pray with Evans Kidero,
then governor of Nairobi, Kenya.

The two women on either side of me are the Honorable Rebecca
Kadaga (right), former speaker of Uganda's parliament, and her fellow
parliament member Cecilia Ogwal. I met with them and members of
their staffs when I visited Uganda to host an evangelistic event.

I met with Ifeanyi Arthur Okowa, governor of Delta State in
Nigeria. We prayed together in his office after a cabinet meeting.

In Ghana I prayed with ancestral leaders during our crusade.

Whenever I blow the shofar, as I'm doing at this evangelistic outreach, I am prophetically announcing the kingdom of God. Assisting me here is Matthew Hartman, who frequently travels with me.

Somehow this little guy ended up resting on my lap during one of our crusades in Uganda.

On this visit to Israel, I was able to preach Yeshua at a Messianic congregation in Jerusalem and participate in the celebration of the Torah.

Cynthia and me with our daughters, Alyssa (left) and Summer, in Israel

God has given me a great leadership team at Discovering the Jewish Jesus. They posed here during a trip to New York (from left): Dustin Roberts, executive producer; Steve Howard, marketing director; Michael Hardy, chief operating officer; Sherri Hardy, communications director; Dave Burkley and John Schmidt, senior editors; Matthew Hannah, my security detail; me; Cynthia; and Summer.

It was a tremendous honor when Cynthia and I received a plaque from the president of the Jerusalem Holocaust Association while in Jerusalem.

Discovering the Jewish Jesus led an evangelistic campaign in Times Square, where we purchased billboards directing people to a website at which I challenged Jewish people to consider that Jesus is the Messiah. Below: This billboard asks, "Is there more than this?" Those words are followed by "WhoAmI.com."

I had the great joy of celebrating Hanukkah in Abakaliki, Nigeria, in 2019.

When Yeshua first revealed Himself to me, I had no idea what was in store. Not only did He bring breakthrough in my life, but He has used me to help others around the world experience breakthrough. What a privilege!

13

A PLACE TO STAND

TOCCOA FALLS AGREED to transfer many of my credits from the University of Tampa and Ohio State, so I was set to graduate in the spring of 1985 if it all went well. I majored in Bible theology. It was a curriculum designed to equip me to become a pastor. We bought a trailer home in Cornelia, Georgia, for about $3,500. Cornelia was about halfway between Toccoa Falls and Gainesville, where Cynthia got a job as a nurse, so we each had about a thirty-minute drive.

The wind blew right through that trailer, so we wore coats indoors all winter. And there was no air conditioning, so in the summertime it got to well over a hundred degrees in there. But we were young and easily able to adapt.

When I showed up for my first day of classes, I looked like I was from another planet. I was twenty-five years old and serious. Almost all the other students were eighteen or nineteen and were, relatively speaking, kids out from under parental authority for the first time and looking to have fun. It was not that there weren't other serious students there, but I was in a league all my own, with few exceptions. I showed up to college that first day with my suit, tie, and briefcase. I mean, I was a man on a mission. I was there to be prepared by God so He could use me for His purposes.

I felt God confirm my decision to go to Bible college during my first spring break, when Cynthia and I went to Florida to visit her mom and dad at their condominium. Several other of Cynthia's family members were there as well. I was taking a nap one afternoon, and while I was lying in bed, the Spirit of the Lord said these three words to me audibly: "Ascend the day." I've never forgotten it. The fact that He had spoken to me gave me confidence that I was in His will.

What I felt the Lord was saying to me was, "Whatever you face, every single day, you can and will ascend it as you cling to Me. I'm going to give you the power to rise above whatever you are facing, just like I raised Jesus from the dead. You'll have victory in your life—*ascend the day.*"

I'm not saying there are no hard days. For me every day is hard in some way because we are in a spiritual war with the powers of darkness. I am also constantly trying to overcome and break through some new barrier in my life or ministry. It simply means that at the end of the day there's something in us that is stronger than anything that we will face in life, both internally and externally.

> In all these things we overwhelmingly conquer through Him who loved us. For I am convinced that neither death, nor life, nor angels, nor principalities, nor things present, nor things to come, nor powers, nor height, nor depth, nor any other created thing, will be able to separate us from the love of God, which is in Christ Jesus our Lord.
>
> —ROMANS 8:37–39

There is a banner of victory over the lives of God's elect, declaring, "But thanks be to God, who always leads us in triumph in Christ, and manifests through us the sweet aroma of the knowledge of Him in every place" (2 Corinthians 2:14). "Ascending the day." It's our calling.

Despite the Lord speaking to me during spring break, I still had a lot of rough edges that needed to be smoothed out. Sometimes I think the only reason they didn't kick me out was because I was the only fully Jewish person in the whole Bible college. Most of the students were well-mannered pastors' and missionaries' kids, and here I was this colorful, uninhibited Jew who had not been raised in their Christian culture and who didn't always know the boundaries. For the most part I did not cause any trouble, but my tongue was still sometimes untamed. Most of my professors were gracious, though. One of my professors confided that the teaching staff thought I was a diamond in the rough. But I am sure that for some of them, I was less diamond and more rough.

Despite rubbing some people the wrong way, I was elected chaplain for our class. There was one professor who was a big guy—probably six four—a John Wayne–type, and he was a former missionary who was now the head of the school's missions department. I don't think he liked me much. (I don't know what he thought for sure—maybe that I was too much of a freewheeler.) I don't think he appreciated my Jewish personality.

One day, I came to school with a black button-down shirt, and I folded up a small sheet of white paper and put it in my collar to make it look like I was a priest. When I walked by, I saw our student class president, who was a friend of mine, talking with this missions professor. Unbeknownst to me my friend was talking with this missions professor and defending me (because the missions professor was telling him I was a disgrace and that I shouldn't be the class chaplain) when I walked by. Later that day, my friend, the class president, told me, "We were talking about you when you walked by. He was saying you are a disgrace, and I was defending you, and then all of a sudden, you walk by dressed up like a priest." All he could do was look down and shake his head in exasperation.

What was amazing and made me happy, though, was how well I excelled academically at Toccoa Falls. I had never been a great student in the past, but once I was in Bible college, studying something I loved, I often tested out with the highest grade in the whole class. But while God blessed me with a real capacity to learn and demonstrate that through my exams, I could get under some of my professors' skin. I was always asking questions, some of which were hard to answer and which they preferred to be unasked because they didn't know the answers or how to reply.

I remember one class in particular in which I was always raising my hand and asking the teacher some deep but hard-to-answer question. I knew I was getting on his nerves, but I almost felt like I couldn't stop myself. I have such a passion for the truth that I have a hard time with pat answers that gloss over things. This same teacher would usually post the name of the top performing student on the department's bulletin board after a major exam. When I got the highest mark in the class, my name was not posted. I guess that's the price you sometimes pay for being a pain in the neck.

It was at this Bible school that I first heard any significant teaching on the personhood and ministry of the Holy Spirit. One of my professors, who was also the dean of the theology department, had us listen to a series of tapes of a man delivering people of demons. You could literally hear the demons coming out. I was fascinated and creeped out at the same time.

The man taught that most of the people he cast demons out of had become possessed when they tried to speak in tongues. (See 1 Corinthians 12 and 14.) Not someone who spoke in tongues himself, this deliverance minister made it sound like opening yourself up to receive the gift of tongues was an invitation to the powers of darkness, which made me very leery of speaking in tongues.

However, there was another student who was a friend of mine and had a different perspective on this. He was the exception, not the rule. One day he invited Cynthia and me over to have dinner with him and his wife. There was something different about this guy—in a good way—that I couldn't exactly put my finger on. I was drawn to him—he had a good spirit. We just connected.

When we got together, he started explaining the gift of speaking in tongues using the Bible as the foundation for his arguments. As he spoke about the biblical perspective regarding speaking in tongues and how it was still for today, I felt the Spirit of God confirm what he was saying. I could just feel that what he was telling me was true. I had a definite inner witness. In the midst of him explaining these things to me, he stopped and looked at me. "What are you feeling right now?" he asked me.

"Nothing," I lied. I was too scared to admit God was confirming what he said about speaking in tongues because of what I'd learned in class, and I'm sure my pride also had something to do with my response. The discussion kind of fizzled out after that, but I never forgot the witness of the Holy Spirit I sensed as he shared what the Scriptures teach about the gift of tongues.

Despite my reluctance, God was going to continue to teach me about the Holy Spirit and what He could—and would—do for us as we allow Him to work in our lives.

Another example of how the Lord continued to train me in the gifts of the Holy Spirit involved a dog. While attending Bible school and living in the trailer in Cornelia, Cynthia and I got a little beagle puppy. There was a little fenced area where we would let him run around, and one day he dug under the fence and ran away. I looked all over the trailer park and saw no sign of him. I had no idea where else to look. After he had been gone for three days, I thought we'd never see him again. The trailer park was near a freeway, and we feared the worst.

Then about two months later I had a dream. In the dream I found our beagle puppy. I remembered the dream vividly the next morning. Then that same day, out of the blue, a farmer about eight miles away called and told us he'd found our dog. He'd gotten our phone number off the tag on the dog's collar and wanted to let us know he was OK. We went and picked him up.

I was blown away that God showed me the future in a dream. As a result, from that day on I started paying very close attention to my dreams and often recorded them in a journal.

Bible school seemed to whiz by, and before I knew it, I was approaching graduation. One of the awards given to graduating seniors was the Preacher of the Year award. I wanted to win that award so much that I had a blue T-shirt made that simply said, "I'm going to win." I didn't tell anybody what it meant. I didn't make it for anyone else. It was a faith declaration between just me and the Lord that I was going to win that award. I'm not sure why it was so important to me, but I wore that shirt about once a week.

Then one day another student came up to me and said, "God

told me you're supposed to give me that shirt." I looked at him a bit upset and confused, but I wasn't going to say no to God, so I gave it to him. It bummed me out, but I tried to forget about it. Then the next week the guy brought it back and told me a bit sheepishly, "Uh, sorry. It's too small." He was considerably bigger than I was. I took it back and thanked him.

Amazingly the weekend of graduation, in May of 1985 in front of a packed auditorium, the head of the Bible theology department called my name, asking me to come forward so I could be presented with the Preacher of the Year award. I felt like God's little boy. The next day, Franklin Graham, evangelist Billy Graham's son, spoke at our graduation.

Me with my parents when I graduated from Toccoa Falls Bible College in May 1985

The academic track I took at Toccoa Falls Bible College was designed to equip me to pastor immediately upon graduation, but I felt that maybe I should continue on with my biblical studies. So Cynthia and I moved to St. Louis, Missouri, in order to start summer school at Covenant Theological Seminary, which was affiliated with the PCA—the Presbyterian Church in America—a conservative evangelical offshoot of the Presbyterian

Church. The presbytery of the PCA in northeast Georgia was going to sponsor me and pay for my tuition, but I felt like I was standing on shaky ground. When I went before the committee the presbytery had formed to interview candidates whom they were considering sponsoring, I was asked to share how I came to faith in Jesus. When I told the head of the committee that Jesus had appeared to me in a vision, he became condescending.

The committee's job was to make a recommendation to the entire presbytery as to whether to sponsor a candidate through seminary. When it was time to make a recommendation one way or the other concerning me, the committee chairman did something irregular. Instead of making a recommendation, he told me to share my testimony with the entire presbytery, which was made up of all the PCA pastors who were part of this northeast Georgia conference. I shared my testimony, and as soon as I was done, one of the elder statesmen among this group of pastors stood up and boldly said, "I wish every Jew and every Muslim would have a vision of Jesus." As a result the vote fell in my favor, but I was concerned about what would happen if in several years, when it was time for me to be ordained, the man who stood up on my behalf was not there. Even though I didn't label myself as charismatic at the time, I knew many of the pastors in the group were anticharismatic and skeptical of supernatural experiences like my vision of Jesus, so I felt I was standing on a shaky foundation with this group. Nevertheless Cynthia and I decided to proceed.

We sold the trailer to a fireman in our community who offered to pay us half up front and half later. Being very naive and not at all business savvy yet, I signed the title over to him with only half the money paid. I thought, "He's a fireman. Surely I can trust him." We got to St. Louis and started getting settled in, and I waited for him to send me the rest of the money. It never came.

Thankfully my brother, Mitchell, was an attorney by that time and just so happened to specialize in real estate law. He wrote a stern and somewhat threatening letter to the guy, and the money arrived quickly. That was a huge lesson to me. I realized that in business you have to do things by the book, even with people you trust. It protects everybody, preserves relationships, and alleviates problems.

I started classes soon after arriving in St. Louis, but it didn't take me long to realize I'd had enough with schooling, not to mention that I felt I was on shaky ground with the PCA. So I decided to forego seminary and start pastoring immediately. I called different superintendents in the CMA, the denomination my Bible school was associated with, and told them I would like to start pastoring. The way the CMA was structured was that the United States was divided into different geographical areas, and each had its own superintendent. I started calling the superintendents all over the country. There wasn't any area that I ruled out. I called them all.

I asked each superintendent if there were any openings. The first superintendent who expressed interest in me was from Montana. He had a group of cattle ranchers who needed a pastor, and there was a mobile home sitting in the middle of some vast piece of acreage for us to live in. It was a little too much of a stretch for this suburban Jewish boy from Cleveland, even if I did like the idea of wearing a cowboy hat.

I kept looking. Next a superintendent in Minnesota was interested. He had a young group in Litchfield who needed a pastor. "They're planting a church and need a pastor," he said. "Right now it's being overseen by one of the teachers at our Bible college in Minneapolis, who's been driving there every week, but now they want to hire a full-time pastor, so you'd be their first pastor."

It sounded like a good fit, so I agreed to go there and interview for the position. The day after the interview, I got a call from the superintendent. They wanted me to come and shepherd the congregation.

Cynthia and I were excited! I accepted the position, and we made plans to move to Minnesota.

14

"YOU ARE AN EVANGELIST"

THERE WAS A core group of about twenty-five people in the CMA church plant in Litchfield, almost all of them in their twenties and thirties. They were committed and passionate. After accepting the post, Cynthia and I contacted a real estate agent to find us a place to live. She found us a trailer we could afford to rent, so we packed a moving van and headed north.

The drive from St. Louis to Litchfield was scary. I don't remember how long the truck we rented was, but it was the longest truck the rental company had available, and I was towing my car behind it. Every time we entered the freeway from an on-ramp or had to switch lanes, my heart was screaming in terror as I prayed I wouldn't hit anybody. Praise God, we made it safely to our trailer home on the outskirts of a cornfield in Litchfield.

While we were still unloading the truck and carrying our possessions into the trailer, the individual who had up to that point been the president of the church board came over to meet with us. He owned his own business and wanted my office to be in his building. He was just a little older than I was and seemed friendly when I met him a few weeks earlier during the interview process.

In CMA churches, pastors are by constitution the president of the board, but this guy had come over to tell us that he planned to remain the board president. When I pointed out that wasn't the way the CMA worked, he countered with, "Well, we're not officially a CMA church." Because they were still a church plant, they had not yet officially registered as a CMA congregation. It was clear he didn't want to give up leadership, and I could tell almost instantly the dynamics were going to be all wrong for me to effectively pastor this group. This guy didn't want a pastor; he just wanted a preacher, and he was not going to be happy if he didn't get his own way. In effect he wanted to run the congregation and use me as a gun for hire to teach and preach.

Well, our adventures in Litchfield had just begun. After he left, Cynthia and I continued to move our things in, and I saw a big rat come out from behind the furnace inside the trailer. We heard him running around in the walls that night. We set out traps to catch him, but he evaded us. One day I heard him and jumped out of my bed after him. He ran down the narrow trailer's hallway into the kitchen, then literally jumped over the trap I had laid beside the refrigerator. Next we tried rat killer, pouring it down one of the holes he was coming in through. We never did catch or kill that thing.

It would prove to be a metaphor for our time there. The guy who wouldn't step down from his position as head of the board turned out to be just as difficult to pin down. When I called the superintendent to tell him about the man, the superintendent decided to drive down from Minneapolis to Litchfield to observe one of our board meetings for himself. Sure enough, the guy elected not to sit at the head of the boardroom table for the first time. Then the next board meeting, when the superintendent was not there, sure enough, there he was, already seated at the head of the table when I walked in the door. I called our superintendent and told him what was happening, and he agreed that we hadn't gotten off on the right foot. But he didn't know what to do about it because he was two hours away, and as an unaffiliated church plant, the congregation was not officially under his authority.

I decided to cut my ties and look for another church. In just a few days a superintendent in western Pennsylvania told us he had a post that involved pastoring two small churches at the same time, one in Reynoldsville and a second church in Falls Creek, seven miles away. Both groups had their own buildings and had been established for some time. The congregation in Litchfield met once a week at a community center they rented. So the fact that these two small churches in Pennsylvania had their own buildings seemed like a step forward. I know a church is much more than the facility where it meets, but when Cynthia and I drove up to the church in Reynoldsville and saw a building with the church name on a sign out front, it seemed more legitimate than our previous post. It was more like what Cynthia and I envisioned when we set out to pastor. We wouldn't be meeting in a community center. We would be meeting in a "real" church.

There were about fifty people in the congregation in Reynoldsville. Unfortunately we soon realized that approximately 75 percent of that congregation were all part of the same family. Falls Creek had about forty members, fewer of whom were related.

After interviewing with both churches, I called the superintendent, who was eagerly waiting to find out how it went. "Sir,"

I said, "do you maybe have anything a little more suburban for me?"

He was quiet for a few seconds. "Well, not right now. But you should think of this like classical music. If you can learn how to play classical music, you'll be able to play any kind of music you want. It gives you the basic skills for every other kind of music. In the same way, if you learn how to pastor these churches, you'll be able to pastor any kind of church down the road." That didn't really settle me, but I had no other options on the horizon. "It might be a good place to grow," I tried to tell myself. We took the assignment.

Cynthia and me in Reynoldsville, Pennsylvania, outside our first "real" church

Looking back, those two churches were a humorous experience where we cut our teeth for sure. The piano player was never there on time and would run in after the service had already begun. The congregation had many senior citizens who easily got cold, so they always had the temperature in the auditorium turned up to about seventy-six degrees, I guess so they could sleep more comfortably while I was preaching. We were there for two years before I began to feel we needed to find another appointment. I remember having a dream in those last months in which I was yelling at God, "You call this a church?" When that happened, I knew it was time to move on.

The best thing that happened in Reynoldsville was that my oldest daughter, Alyssa, was born. Even as a child she had a supernatural anointing of God upon her. I remember one day looking at her and seeing the Spirit of the Lord in and through her. Father has used Alyssa in my life in many ways, including giving me prophetic words on more than one occasion. One dream she had resulted in a geographical move that Cynthia and I made.

The next church we went to pastor was, thankfully, back in Ohio. The Fremont, Ohio, congregation ran about a hundred, and it had much more diversity and life than any of the churches we had led up to that point. It was the first place where we really felt at home and like we were appreciated. The church grew while we were there, and we built a bigger building so we could continue to grow. When it was finished, our new building was one of the nicest in Fremont.

We hadn't been long in Fremont when Father God spoke audibly to me once again. This time I was standing in a hospital waiting room. My mother-in-law had had an aneurysm, and Cynthia and I rushed to Cleveland, where she was having surgery. Standing alone in the waiting room, I literally heard the voice of Father God speak to me from heaven. It was forceful and clear as a bell. He said, "You are an evangelist." This was not a voice I perceived but again one that I plainly and distinctly heard; I heard the word of the Lord.

I was pastoring, so God telling me I was an evangelist confused and concerned me. Was I not supposed to be pastoring? Was I doing something wrong? In my mind evangelists were guys who went to busy street corners with a lot of foot traffic and handed out gospel tracts. Was God telling me I was supposed to step down as a pastor and hand out tracts? I needed illumination and clarification.

Since I knew that God had spoken, I kept looking to Him for direction. I searched through the Scriptures and read every passage where the word *evangelist* appeared. Philip had been called "the evangelist" in Acts 21:8. I read in Ephesians 4:11–12 that evangelists are one of the fivefold ministry gifts that help build the church: "He gave some as apostles, and some as prophets, and some as evangelists, and some as pastors and teachers, for the equipping of the saints for the work of service, to the building up of the body of Christ." Still I didn't have clarity. So I looked into the etymology of the word. I found out that an evangelist is one who brings good news. I thought, "Well, I'm doing that, Lord. I'm preaching the good news of Messiah [the gospel] every week as a pastor."

I still didn't feel completely at peace, but at least I didn't feel like I had to make an immediate change. I will share more about this later, but I eventually realized God wasn't telling me not to pastor, just that my main calling was to be an evangelist. It was something like Paul in Scripture; he was a preacher, an apostle, and a teacher. (See 1 Timothy 2:7.) Many pastors I know are both teachers and evangelists. I came to understand that I am an evangelist first but also a teacher with an apostolic anointing.

But there was another door that needed to be opened in order for me to enter more fully into my evangelistic calling.

The Lord was about to take me into the biggest breakthrough I had experienced in my life since Jesus had appeared to me in my dream. It was time for me to get better acquainted with the Holy Spirit.

15

THE HOLY SPIRIT

IMMEDIATELY UPON MOVING into our new building in Fremont, I experienced the Lord powerfully drawing me into a deeper relationship with the Holy Spirit. I was searching, and I didn't feel I was making fast enough progress in getting closer to Him. I knew there was more of God. What was I missing?

I began a systematic pursuit. When I wanted to become the best wrestler in my state, I made a chart of all the disciplines I felt I needed to practice every week to improve. But in my quest to get closer to Father, I reached a place where I felt I had done everything I knew to do. I was praying every day, studying the Word, reading books, listening to messages, and talking with other pastors, all in hopes of gaining an insight. It seemed as if every book, every service, every sermon ended the same way: We should read the Bible more. We should spend more time in prayer. We should witness more, and we should give tithes and offerings, or give beyond the tithe if we were already tithing.

These were all good things, and I was doing them all to the nth degree. I mean, if I was in line at the grocery store and turned around and saw someone behind me, I would witness to the person. If I passed someone while walking on the sidewalk, I'd stop him or her. I thought I might never see the person again, so that may have been the only chance I would ever have to share Jesus with him or her. Over the years, I've given my Bible away more times than I've been able to keep track of—I don't mean just giving out Bibles but giving away the brand-new Bible I'd bought for myself because I felt strongly that the person I had just witnessed to needed it. I could always get another, but here was this person I just witnessed to who needed it right then.

The point is that I was doing everything I thought I should do to grow closer to God. And I was starting to feel a bit burned out, like nothing I was doing was bringing me into the intimate experience of God's presence that I was looking for.

Then I discovered a prayer method called, "Could you not tarry one hour?" It was based on using what is often referred to as the Lord's Prayer (also sometimes called the Disciple's Prayer) in Matthew 6:9–13 as an outline to pray for one hour. You'd start, "Our Father, who is in heaven, hallowed be Your *name*," and then you'd spend time going through all the names of God in the Old Testament and praising Him for the aspects of His personality that each name represented. For example, Yahweh Yireh (Jehovah Jireh) means God our Provider, Yahweh Rapha (Jehovah Rapha) means God our Healer, Yahweh Nissi (Jehovah Nissi) means the Lord our Banner, and so on. You would declare, for example, "Father, thank You for being my provider. I praise You Yahweh Yireh (Jehovah Jireh)," and so on. Then you'd pray that His kingdom would come and so on through the Lord's Prayer, praying after every line to make it personal.

I started out praying this way for fifteen minutes a day. Nothing changed. I increased it to a half hour, and nothing changed. I increased it to an hour a day, then an hour and a half, then two hours. Nothing, nothing, nothing changed. I increased it to three hours a day—and I should note that my mindset was that if I wasn't literally speaking to God with my mouth moving and sounds coming out, it didn't count. Still nothing changed, and I grew more exasperated and discouraged. Then I thought, "Well, maybe I'm talking *too* much. I'll try praying out loud for an hour and a half and then listening for an hour and a half." Again nothing changed. In desperation I said to myself, "Tomorrow I'm just going to sit here and try to listen and wait on God for three hours."

I fell asleep.

That broke me. I had tried everything. I didn't know what to do. I'd done everything I knew to do, and I still didn't feel any closer to God or feel His presence any more than I had when I started.

After I came to the end of myself with all my efforts, the Holy Spirit spoke to me. It wasn't an audible voice but something I perceived clearly in my heart and mind. I sensed Him telling me, "I want you to stop praying about all the things you've been praying about, and I want you to ask Me for just this one thing: Ask Me to give you revelation of the fact that I live inside you— that Christ is *in you*, the hope of glory." (See Colossians 1:27.)

So I did. And from that day on *I have experienced a new power in my life!*

As this revelation grew, an awakening took place inside me. I was waking up to God's presence within me. He was now becoming more and more of a reality to me.

As this revelation was taking root in me, I also came to the realization that I had started speaking in tongues (1 Corinthians 14:1–5) without even realizing I was doing it. I know that seems hard to understand, but here is what happened. When I got really burdened by something, I just began to speak to God in words that were not in English or any other known language, just as the Scriptures describe: "the Spirit Himself intercedes for us with groanings too deep for words" (Romans 8:26). It was like a transmission automatically shifting to a lower gear, as it would if the car were going up a steep hill—like kicking into overdrive. Speaking in tongues wasn't something I cognitively initiated or was trying to do; I didn't even know what it was at first. It was only later that I started thinking, "I think this is the gift of tongues. This is the prayer language of the Spirit that Paul wrote about in 1 Corinthians 14:2: 'For one who speaks in a tongue does not speak to men but to God; for no one understands, but in his spirit he speaks mysteries.'"

When I later realized I could speak in tongues at will, I thought it couldn't be real since I could do it whenever I wanted. It confused me. I didn't have any specific direction or teaching about speaking in tongues; it was just something that began to happen supernaturally. I didn't tell anyone about it and only prayed that way when I was alone in my office. I eventually came to understand that what I was experiencing truly was what the Scriptures were talking about in 1 Corinthians 14, and a peace settled over me.

During this time, I was also moving into a deeper realm of being able to understand and interpret my dreams. God had spoken to me in dreams and visions before, some of which I've already shared, but it was during this time that I saw more clearly what the Bible had to say about them. In Acts 2:17–18 Peter quoted the Book of Joel, saying:

> "And it shall be in the last days," God says, "that I will pour forth of My Spirit on all mankind; and your sons and your daughters shall prophesy, and your young men shall see

visions, and your old men shall dream dreams; even on My bondslaves, both men and women, I will in those days pour forth of My Spirit and they shall prophesy."

I saw clearly that God's purpose is to regularly communicate with His New Testament church in this way. When I realized this, I got even more deliberate about recording my dreams in my dream journal, where I would write down any dreams that struck me as significant.

As I shared more of the supernatural with my very conservative congregation, some questioned it. An older gentleman, a farmer who was about seventy-five, spoke out during one of our Wednesday evening prayer meetings. He stood, pointed his finger at me, and said, "If you got it, I ain't seen it." He was a solid and respected member of the congregation but very stubborn, set in his ways, and opinionated.

There were other leaders, too, who said to me, "Pastor, everybody loves your preaching. Just preach like you used to, and don't say anything else." They were not ready to accept the supernatural as the intimate reality that is for today. They just wanted to study how God supernaturally worked in the lives of the Bible characters. It was OK that God spoke to and did miracles for Moses, Elijah, Jacob, Peter, and Paul, but they were closed off to God working like that in believers' lives today.

Rather than calming their concerns, I pushed things to the brink. One Sunday while preaching, in an effort to help the people of the congregation understand that we can have a relationship with the living God, I did something that I probably wouldn't do today. I lifted my Bible before the congregation and said, "This Bible is not God." Then I dropped it on the ground and pointed to heaven. "God is God." I wasn't trying to diminish the Scriptures in any way. Those who are familiar with my ministry know that I am a Word teacher. I root everything I say in the Scriptures, the written Word of God.

I was just trying to tell people that the God who wrote the Bible is alive and that we need to seek the living God. We need to go beyond just reading about and studying what He did for other people. We need to believe and expect Him to work in our lives in the present time. Jesus said to the Pharisees, "You search the Scriptures because you think that in them you have eternal life; it is these that testify about Me; and you are unwilling to come to Me so that you may have life" (John 5:39–40). Yeshua, in this verse, was dealing with the same phenomenon in His day that I was facing in the church I was pastoring.

But many in the congregation saw my action as disrespecting the Scriptures, and the church board called the district superintendent about what I'd done. He immediately called me and told me not to go to the evening service and that he was driving in to see me the next day. Again, looking back, perhaps I should have found a different way to communicate this truth, but I still had a little too much youthful brashness at the time.

When the superintendent arrived, I said, "Truth is truth. I'm not backing down." The superintendent told me he thought I should go to counseling. I knew I was experiencing a work of God in my life (even if the expression of it was my own), and I felt like agreeing to get counseling would be backing away from what the Lord was showing me. I couldn't do that. So I told the superintendent, "I'm sorry. I'm not going to do that."

"If you don't, you'll need to step down as pastor," he countered.

"OK," I said. "I'll step down."

I felt it was better to stay with God and trust Him than to compromise and admit defeat. The situation was black and white to me. I felt I had no choice.

We moved out of the parsonage and into a trailer nearby. It was during this season that our second daughter, Summer, was born. Summer is used of the Lord to minister both prophetically and through the gift of wisdom to me personally. Not long ago, when a door closed for me, she had a prophetic word for me that really helped me know that this closed door was part of God's plan. It unquestionably strengthened me. Summer thinks a lot like me, and I often turn to both her and Alyssa for advice.

I came to grips with the reality that although the Lord was establishing something deep within me, I also had a lot of growing up to do, and I needed to step away from pastoring. Knowing I needed to support my family but that there was little opportunity in Fremont, I wasn't sure what to do until God spoke to me in a vision of the night. (See Acts 16:9.) In it I saw the word Columbus in rainbow colors and with a rainbow-colored halo around it.

I had no context for it but believed with complete confidence that the Lord had just spoken to me and showed me that I was supposed to move to Columbus, Ohio. So having no job in Columbus and no close relationships there, Cynthia and I again rented a moving truck, loaded up our things, and moved to Columbus. I bought a mobile home in a mobile home park located in one of the poorest sections of the area we moved to and started looking for work.

16

THE BUSINESS WORLD

L IKE MOSES, WHO had to spend time in the desert of Midian before he was fully prepared for the work the God of Israel had for him (Exodus 2:15–3:14), so too were the next several years of my life a desert experience. They appear to be a step backward in my journey, but the Lord was actually establishing and preparing me so that He could send me forth in a special way.

It was the early 1990s when we moved to Columbus. I was thirty-five years old and focused on creating a new path forward for my family. It was a huge adjustment for sure. But Cynthia stood by my side and supported me. Cynthia's mom and dad taught her to be practical and do what it takes to survive. She also has never been focused on money, worldly success, or material things. So she was flexible, and we pressed on together.

I applied for a number of jobs, but the one that felt best was a position with MassMutual Insurance Company as a financial adviser. In the capacity I served, I was functioning as both a salesperson and an adviser. I always had a knack for sales, even as a kid. When I was a seventh grader, every class in Brady Middle

School, where I attended, had to create some kind of carnival booth with games kids would pay fake money to play. The kids were all handed the same number of tickets, which they could use to play games at whatever booths they wanted. Whichever class' booth had the most tickets at the end won a prize. It turns out my class teacher took this very seriously and was very competitive about it, so throughout the day he would send one of his students down to the carnival to monitor how busy our booth was compared with the others. Whenever he became concerned that we were not winning, he would send me down to drum up business. It was the same way when we were sealing driveways—I was the salesman who got us the jobs.

Being a financial adviser was a stretch because I was young and did not have a sophisticated grasp of financial tools, but I learned quickly. I became MassMutual's number one producer in the country—out of all of their new agents—for my first six months with them. Right off the bat, though, I didn't feel it was enough to just be an insurance salesman. So I decided to get registered with the state as an investment adviser. Other agents in my office thought I was crazy for doing that—they were afraid to be accountable to a federal agency, the Securities and Exchange Commission, for the advice they gave. Becoming a registered investment adviser wasn't required, so to them it was a hoop they didn't need to jump through, something that just made things more difficult. But it was something I felt I should do, so I filled out all the paperwork, submitted what was required, and got the credentials.

In the meantime, Cynthia, the girls, and I found a church that was more open to the things of the Spirit and had strong worship. One thing I started to lose was any pretense of trying to be religious. Some of the airs I'd affected while pastoring started to fall away. Now I wasn't a pastor trying to model what I thought pastors should be or look like. I was just me. I think it helped me get more in touch with God and myself, which eventually led me to a deeper inner cleansing and transformation as well as prepared me to minister to others more authentically. It was a subtle breakthrough but an important one.

All the while, I never stopped talking about what Jesus had done in my life and how God had revealed Himself to me. In this season, I wasn't as disciplined as I was while I was pastoring in reading my Bible, praying, and so on, but my heart was still questing to enter into His fullness. It wasn't like I had backslidden; I was just trying to find my way, and sometimes my steps were not straight ahead.

During this time, I learned a great deal about finances and managing money, particularly while I worked for MassMutual. I also learned a lot about business in those years. Looking back, I'm very thankful for those difficult years because the Lord was building a skill set and knowledge base into my life that would be needed later in the ministry He was preparing for me. Although I was one of MassMutual's top recruits in the country, I wasn't really making much money because though I had a large number of clients, I was doing business with a lot of young people who didn't have much money to invest. Cynthia and I were barely getting by financially. People told me I had to be there for a while before it paid off, but I didn't enjoy the work and wasn't convinced that it would materialize into a successful career. So after three years as a financial adviser, I got a job with a real estate company that specialized in selling new homes. They paid on commission, and since the new builds were high-ticket items, the potential upside of the business was immediately apparent to me.

Not only that but as it turned out, Columbus was the new-home capital of the country at the time, and the company I began working for, MI Homes, was a leading builder. I started making a solid income in a short time, and soon we were able to move out of the trailer park and buy our first home.

After being with MI for about two and a half years, I went to work with another leading builder with a national reputation called Centex. I got along great with the sales manager at Centex, who was also a believer. In fact, I interviewed with him in the afternoon and then surprisingly ran into him a few hours later that night in Columbus at a concert featuring Michael Card, a leading Christian musician at the time. Unfortunately, after a year he was fired and was replaced with the husband of one of our other salespeople. I could read the handwriting on the wall. I was the top salesperson in the Columbus office, and there was considerable jealousy and animosity toward me from some of the other salespeople, including the woman whose husband had become our new sales manager. The day her husband took over, he gathered all the salespeople in the company's conference room and said something like, "If you think you're top dog now, you'd better be looking over your shoulder because someone is behind you coming to take your place."

When my friend who was fired had been the manager, it was common to negotiate the list price in order to close deals. This was accepted practice. Apparently I missed the memo (probably because there wasn't one) that this was no longer acceptable under the new sales manager. When I turned in a deal I had closed through negotiation, my new manager got livid. *Who did I think I was? Who'd authorized me to negotiate and change the price?* I was the top performer, but he didn't care. He wanted me gone from the day he got there because he was threatened by me and because of his wife's animosity toward me. I knew he was going to make it difficult for me and probably try to fire me in the near future, so I resigned before he got the chance. I wanted to exit while I was on top so I could feel good about myself and empowered for whatever was next.

I want to say before going on that the reason I was a skilled salesperson is because the Lord gifted me with communication skills and confidence to put things together. In all of my career positions in sales I always represented the best companies with the best product for the consumer. Ultimately God was preparing me to present Jesus/Yeshua to the world as His evangelist. So all of this experience in the secular world prepared me for the work of being an ambassador for the kingdom of God.

> Therefore, we are ambassadors for Christ, as though God were making an appeal through us; we beg you on behalf of Christ, be reconciled to God.
>
> —2 Corinthians 5:20

After leaving Centex, I wanted to start my own business. I had worked so hard to become the top salesperson there, only to have it taken away in a second when the sales management changed. I wanted more control so this couldn't happen to me again. My options to be self-employed were few since I didn't have much cash to use as startup capital. I did a lot of research on businesses I could start for less than $25,000, but I didn't see much that intrigued me. In the meantime I had stayed in touch with my previous sales manager at Centex, and he told me about a multilevel marketing company that had bought the name Rexall, a drug store chain that had as many as ten thousand stores.[1] (They are now very rare, having been replaced by massive chains like CVS.)

My friend said he and his neighbor, an emergency room physician, were working with Rexall, which had a line of nutraceuticals that had proved to be effective in many cases. In particular, it had a fiber product that numerous medical studies had demonstrated lowered cholesterol. Because I believed in my friend's professionalism and integrity, and because we were both being mentored by his neighbor who was a licensed MD, I decided to move forward.

I did this for about a year and rose up quickly through their ranks, but I soon realized none of the people I was recruiting were making any money. Once I realized that, I couldn't keep recruiting people in good faith, so I got out.

Once again it was only the grace of God that was keeping me afloat.

17

JESUS IS WHAT I HAVE TO OFFER

W
ITH NO NEW prospects on the horizon, I turned to the help wanted ads in the newspaper and came across a rare opportunity with a motivational speaking company. It was actually the first time in many years that I had looked in that section of the paper for a job, and *bam*! Here was a job right up my alley.

The company was called Yes! A Positive Network (now called The YES! Network), and it was looking for a representative in Ohio. The job was to go to businesses that had sales teams of roughly twelve to fifty people and offer to give a free motivational seminar. The idea was to show them the value of motivational seminars—that they could help improve their staffs' productivity—and then sell them a package of eight motivational talks that their salespeople could attend over the next year for $299. The job seemed like a very good fit since I was already a very successful salesperson and had strong communication skills.

I was soon doing a considerable amount of driving to give talks, and I was on the road a lot. So to empower myself, I came up with the idea of creating cassette tapes on which I'd record all the words of Jesus in the New Testament with my own voice so I could listen to His words over and over again as I drove. Jokingly I came to call them my "drink and drive" tapes because I was drinking in God's Word while driving. At first they were just for me—I didn't have any plans for them beyond edifying myself as I drove. Listening to Jesus' words over and over again brought me deeper into God's peace and the pulse of His heart.

As Jesus' words sank into my heart through repetition, I realized my cassette tapes of the words of Jesus in the New Testament could help a lot of other people as well. So I hired a sound engineer to professionally record me reading through the red-letter Scriptures (Jesus' words) in the Gospels, got a graphic artist to design a cover, and made the tapes available to the public.

It didn't matter that I wasn't leading a congregation; God hadn't given up on what He wanted to do with my life. As a result Father continued to break into my life in some dramatic and powerful ways. One night in my sleep I found myself in an encounter with Father's Spirit flowing as a river of fire into my soul and then back to Him in a circular motion. This wasn't a vision or a dream (2 Corinthians 12:3–5) but an encounter with the living God. As this river of fire flowed from the Lord into my soul and then back to Him over and over, it was accompanied by Father's voice saying, "Seize My Word, and don't let anything else in."

I wondered and prayed about exactly what I was supposed to do to obey these words. How could I seize the approximately 800,000 words written in the Bible? Did God mean seize the whole Bible or specific parts? Or was Father telling me to seize the words He had directly spoken to me, like "I am a servant" and "You are an evangelist"? Was He referring to revelations

He had shown me in dreams or visions? Or did it mean seize *the Word*, Jesus, Yeshua, as described in John 1:1 and 14: "In the beginning was the Word, and the Word was with God, and the Word was God....And the Word became flesh, and dwelt among us, and we saw His glory, glory as of the only begotten from the Father, full of grace and truth"?

What I finally arrived at through much searching and prayer is that God's word to me involved all of the above. Whether it's something from the written Word of God, a devotional, or spiritual literature; a revelation the Lord has given us through His Spirit; or something He has taught us through our experiences in life, we should seize it, cling to it, and make it part of who we are.

The truth is, though, that as clear, powerful, and marked as this encounter was, I felt like an utter failure applying it. No matter how much I tried to keep all my thoughts focused on God alone, my mind still wandered. The Lord said to me, "Don't let anything else in," but I still found my mind drifting and thinking about all types of things.

I remember that one time about three years after this encounter, I was sitting down having lunch with a pastor friend of mine, and I was telling him about the divine voice and the river of fire saying to me, "Seize my Word, and don't let anything else in," and I started crying right there in the restaurant. I said, "God said this to me, but I'm not doing it." I was striving to, but I felt I wasn't able.

Over time I have grown in being able to seize, discern, and obey God's Word, but it is still definitely a work in progress. Like all of us, I'm not perfect, but I'm on the road to perfection. As long as we are growing and moving forward, we are successful in bearing fruit. The author of Hebrews said, "But solid food is for the mature, who because of practice have their senses trained to discern good and evil" (Hebrews 5:14). I am being transformed day by day and continuing to strive to seize God's Word and not let anything else in.

As I was continuing to listen to my drink and drive tapes on the way to the places I was to give a motivational seminar, I began to again ponder my career. The motivational talks I had been giving were business oriented to help salespeople be successful. I was representing Yes! A Positive Network as their front man, but I wanted to branch out on my own as a keynote motivational speaker. So I began to ask God, "Lord, what do I have to offer people? What should be my motivational keynote speech?" The first thing I thought of was my expertise with closing sales. I asked myself, "What makes me successful at closing sales?" I realized it was that I had the courage to ask for the sale. So then I asked myself, "What gives me the courage?"

When I asked myself that question, I immediately knew the answer: "Jesus!" My courage came from God.

That revelation led to what has been one of the most critical turning points in my life.

I half laughed in joy and clarity.

It was a breakthrough eureka moment.

It had been nearly a decade since I'd left the pastorate. I thought I was done with pastoring, but suddenly I knew my life's call was to get back out there to proclaim the good news of Messiah Jesus once again. God had after all told me, "You are an evangelist." I recognized that the good news was the best message I had to offer—that knowing God through Messiah Jesus is what people needed, not only to obtain courage but to come into alignment with their Creator and find the abundant life He promised. The gospel was the gift and message I had for the world. My audience was not salespeople but the whole world. I realized that in addition to my own personal transformation, this is why God put me on the earth. I needed to be preaching the gospel.

What I wasn't quite sure of was how. What needed to be my next step?

As I prayed about it, the Lord caused me to understand: "I've called you as a Jew to preach the Jewish Jesus. This is your unique call."

As I've shared already, nothing I'd learned for my Bar Mitzvah had taught me anything about having a personal relationship with God, and very little that I'd gleaned at Bible school had pointed to understanding the New Testament through anything but a Gentile lens. It felt like the New Testament was all that mattered and the Old Testament was only ancient history. It seemed there was no real connection between the two, even though virtually everything Jesus spoke was as a Jew, in a Jewish context, and originally to Jewish people.

The more I thought about that, the more obvious it was that this de-Judaizing of the Christian faith just didn't make sense.

Even though I had attended a Messianic synagogue for a short time before heading off to Bible school, in reality I had very little teaching on the Jewish roots and culture of the New Testament. As I said, there was not much emphasis during my Bible school training on Jesus being a devout Jew. But as I started to read through the Gospels again, Yeshua's words in Matthew 5:17 suddenly leaped off the page to me in a new way: "Do not think that I came to abolish the Law or the Prophets; I did not come to abolish but to fulfill." Jesus was recognized as a rabbi, taught in the synagogues, and celebrated all the Jewish holidays right down to Passover the night before He was crucified.

While I was pondering these things, I learned that there was going to be a convention of Jewish believers in a few weeks' time. People were coming from all over the world to attend, and it was taking place in downtown Columbus. I decided to go.

When I got there, I was full of questions. Not knowing anyone, I'd go up to people randomly, introduce myself, and start asking things like, "I'm Jewish, and I want to start identifying with Jesus as a Jew. How do I do that? What do I do?" I received a variety of answers, but the one that stuck out the most was that I should start celebrating Shabbat. Another common one was that I should start wearing tzitzit—the tassels Jews wear from the four corners of their garments. (See Numbers 15:38–41.) Others suggested I eat kosher. I decided to start with these three.

I want to state here that I have never seen myself nor have I ever attempted to put others under Old Testament Law, as some critics of Messianic Judaism claim. But as a Jew I wanted, and still want, to identify with Jesus as a Jew. (For this reason I now often call Him Yeshua, as He would have been called when He walked the earth.) I want to do this for personal reasons, as well as for the purpose of being a testimony on the earth that declares Yeshua is the Jewish Messiah and that a person can believe in Him and still be Jewish.

I dug deep into the Scriptures and created a powerful, dynamic, and practical message called "The Principle of the Sabbath and the Presence of God." In this message I taught Christians how they could apply the principles of the Sabbath to their own lives without putting themselves under the Law. Before too long I found myself speaking in churches all across the country. I'd go to ministerial association gatherings and teach on this subject; then afterward I would pass around a clipboard for pastors to sign up for me to go to their churches and declare the same message.

The message changed lives. I taught them that keeping the Sabbath wasn't just a commandment but a creation principle going all the way back to the second chapter of the Book of Genesis. God rested on the seventh day. He blessed it and sanctified it. Why did God rest on the seventh day? Was He tired? No. God doesn't get tired. We all know that. He did it because He wanted to model for us how we ought to live life.

In Mark 2:27 Jesus said, "The Sabbath was made for man, and not man for the Sabbath." Beginning in Genesis, I traced the Sabbath, showing what it meant *even before* the Ten Commandments were given. For example, in Exodus 16 God told Israel to gather up twice as much manna on the sixth day because on the seventh day there would be no manna. It was the Sabbath, consecrated to God; there was to be no work. *My goal was not to put us under the Law. My goal was to help God's people understand the importance of setting aside time in our lives that is sanctified and set apart for Him.*

My point was let's not throw out the baby with the bathwater. The Creator wrote the owner's manual for our lives. He knows what we need as human beings. We need to be refreshed in Him. We need to take a day a week to rest in Him so we can become human *beings* and not just human *doings*. We need to be able to set aside a day to honor Him and receive from Him, and we need to put boundaries up in our lives so that our Sabbath is really a day of refreshment in Him. Again, Yeshua said, "The Sabbath was made for man, and not man for the Sabbath" (Mark 2:27). I taught that for New Covenant believers the Sabbath is not about the Law but is an opportunity for spiritual blessing.

Biblically the Sabbath starts Friday at sunset and ends Saturday evening at sundown. (In Judaism the day starts in the evening because in the creation story we read, "And there was evening and there was morning, one day" [Genesis 1:5].) I did not teach on this subject from a legalistic perspective but rather taught believers in Messiah how to apply the principle of the Sabbath to their lives because Paul taught:

> Therefore no one is to act as your judge in regard to food or drink or in respect to a festival or a new moon or a Sabbath day.
> —COLOSSIANS 2:16

As you might expect, the message was revelation for those who heard it, and it blessed those who took it to heart.

When I was done, I would go to the pastor and say, "If you felt my ministry was a blessing for your people, I'd really appreciate it if you could call a couple other pastors that you know and tell them about my ministry. If you're open to that, I'll give you a call in a week, and maybe you could share with me who you were able to connect with."

I was finally ready for God to take me into a new thing. I was back to my calling. I just had no idea how much He had planned for it.

18

DISCOVERING THE JEWISH JESUS

WITHIN A FEW months I was booked out for the next year. The ministry opportunities were just there like flowers to be gathered from a field. I was seeing the first seeds of what would become *Discovering the Jewish Jesus*.

In that first year of splitting time between speaking for Yes! A Positive Network and teaching in churches, a prophetic church invited me to speak, and I was there for three consecutive nights. At the end of my time with them they had a little reception for me with refreshments in the fellowship hall, where I could meet some of the members. As the evening went on, the pastor stood and asked, "OK, does anyone have a word for Kirt?"

Several people stood and said encouraging things but nothing that really struck me as profound until one young lady stood up. She said, "The Lord showed me this simple little wooden boat sitting on the shore of this big ocean. You knew it was your boat, but you didn't know whether it could get you to the other side of that ocean because it was so small and so simple. But that little boat is going to get you to the other side because it's solid and sturdy." From the way the woman described what she saw in the spirit, I could tell it was prophetic because I knew the Lord spoke to me in this same manner—by putting subtle pictures on the screen of my mind to communicate something. I understood through this vision that was shared that the Lord was going to take my simple ministry to faraway places and across oceans.

Now, years later, I literally have seen how Father has used *Discovering the Jewish Jesus* to spread the simple but profound message of Messiah Jesus across the oceans to reach even the far places of the earth. The young woman's vision has come to pass.

Another congregation I visited in that first year was Adat Adonai (Congregation of the Lord), a Messianic synagogue in Toledo, which is a couple of hours north of Columbus. I had a good connection with the rabbi there and enjoyed the people. They asked me to come back to speak a handful of times.

In 2002 the rabbi overseeing Adat Adonai decided to step down for personal reasons, and the congregation remembered me. The director over their area asked if I would fill in for a couple of months. I agreed, and that eventually led to my being their rabbi full-time. Since they met only for Sabbath services, I was able to speak there on Friday nights and Saturday mornings, then elsewhere on Sundays. It was a very good fit. I drove to Toledo on Friday afternoons and then from there to wherever I needed to be for a Sunday church service.

The first time I spoke at Adat Adonai, the cover of their bulletin featured pictures of meat and milk with a red "not" symbol over them. Their message was, "Eat kosher; don't mix meat and milk together." The Jewish community extrapolates this from the verse, "You are not to boil a young goat in the milk of its mother" (Exodus 23:19). My understanding of this verse is that it is communicating the tender and sensitive nature of God's heart, that boiling a goat in the milk of its mother would be unnatural and without respect for the goat's life and the special love a mother has for her young. However, the traditional rabbinic interpretation goes far beyond this simple but profound understanding.

Orthodox Judaism teaches that this verse means that we as Jewish people should never eat dairy and meat products together—not even to use the same plates, silverware, or dishwasher for dairy and meat products. A Jewish home that eats strictly kosher will have separate dishwashers. (In fact, very strict Jewish homes have two completely different kitchens.) The concern is that if you ate meat on a plate and put it in the same dishwasher with a plate that was going to later be used to eat cheese, by accident a microscopic piece of meat might find its way into and get lodged in a pore of your dairy plate. Then the next time you ate cheese or some dairy product on your dairy plate, you would inadvertently consume a microscopic piece of meat that had gotten lodged there while being washed alongside dishes that had been used for eating meat and thus end up breaking the rabbinic prohibition of not eating milk and meat together. Unfortunately I ran into some Messianic believers—Jews who believe in Jesus and Gentiles who self-identify as Messianic because they want to reclaim the Hebrew roots of Christianity—who held this type of thinking. To me, they were emphasizing the wrong things, leaning more toward keeping the Law than finding freedom in Yeshua.

I found that some Messianic groups emphasize the Law and rabbinic traditions more than following Yeshua and being led by the Holy Spirit. Some Gentiles would join these congregations to become Jewish devotees rather than devoted followers of Yeshua. They romanticized Judaism and wanted to be a part of God's chosen people. They wanted to dress Jewish, act Jewish, look

Jewish, and do Jewish things. At times this caused some to lose focus on keeping Jesus at the center of their lives. Instead they became obsessed with Rabbinism—trying to live like traditional Jews even though they weren't Jewish. My focus has always been to point people, whether Jew or Gentile, to Jesus, not romance them into living like traditional religious Jews.

One funny story I remember involved a Gentile who was already part of Adat Adonai when I got there. He was one of these guys who grew up as a Gentile but suddenly wanted to be Jewish. He started wearing tzitzit—fringes (Numbers 15:38)—that he made out of yarn and tied to his belt loops (definitely not the prescribed or kosher way to wear them). I was friends with his previous pastor, who was pastoring a traditional congregation nearby, and I asked him to fill in for me one day when I was going to be out of town. So his previous pastor showed up at Adat Adonai and this guy, wearing his yarn *tzitzit*, went up to him and said, "You're not going to make us stop being Jewish, are you?" His previous pastor looked at him and said, "Dude, you're not Jewish!" When I heard about the incident from the pastor who filled in for me, I thought it was very funny! I've dealt with a lot of crazy stuff!

I also observed that some were more concerned with being accepted and affirmed by the traditional Jewish community than they were with following Yeshua. The truth is that Messianic Jews like myself will never be accepted by the traditional Jewish community until Messiah breaks in. As soon as you mention Jesus, you are out. It is the same today as it was in Yeshua's day, as recorded in John 9:22: "For the Jews had already agreed that if anyone confessed Him [Yeshua] to be Christ, he was to be put out of the synagogue."

As I started emphasizing Yeshua at Adat Adonai and

deemphasizing rabbinic laws and manmade traditions, a group rose up in rebellion and loudly expressed their discontent with the changes I was making. Eventually this group left, but I wasn't concerned because I realized I needed to build the congregation on the right foundation. I wanted people who were dedicated to Yeshua above all else and who supported the direction we were going. I was like, "We've lost some people, but *baruch Hashem* (Blessed be the name of the Lord), we're going to start over and build on the rock of Yeshua." So we began to rebuild the congregation with more of a balanced ministry—centered on Yeshua, teaching the Judaic roots of our faith, and following the leading of the Holy Spirit.

My message was and still is that Yeshua fulfilled, not supplanted, the Old Testament. It's about Yeshua being the Messiah of Israel and Savior of the world, not the creator of a new religion. He is the one true path to God and the culmination of God's plan that began with Abraham and continued through Isaac, Jacob, and David. I taught the importance of living by the life of the Spirit as opposed to living in the flesh or returning to legalism. It took us a few years to weather these controversies, but we got to a point where we had about forty to fifty people who were on board with the truth, and we started rebuilding and growing from there.

Sometime early on during my pastorate at Adat Adonai, God spoke to me in another dream. I saw a person, and I somehow knew he was God's favorite preacher. I didn't see his face in the dream; I just somehow knew that he was God's best and favorite preacher. I instantly wanted to know what made this man so special. Why was He Father's choicest preacher?

I began following him all over in my dream, trying to discover what made him so special to God. Finally, as I followed him, I was led down into the basement of a home. It was simple and unfinished, with concrete block walls and a cement floor—bare bones, nothing fancy at all. In the middle of the basement was a raw wooden table. On the table was what looked like a soup can with no label on it. Somehow I knew that inside that soup can was the answer I was looking for—whatever made that man God's favorite and best preacher was written on a piece of paper inside that can.

As I reached into the can to pull out the answer, the Spirit of the Lord spoke clearly to me in the dream and said, "You know that it was My Word that saved you, and you will never betray Me."

Hearing the Lord speak that to me solidified me. God assured me that I will preach the truth because I know in my inner being, in the deepest parts of my nature, what He saved me from and how He did it. I knew when the Spirit said, "My Word," He meant not only the written Word of God but also the living Word, Yeshua, Jesus. And to hear Father say, "You will never betray Me," has brought me security that is not of this world, because He assured me that He'd put something in me so deep that I will stay anchored and be faithful to Him until the end, by His grace, amen.

As the congregation continued to grow and develop at Adat Adonai, I got an interesting opportunity to start teaching a thirty-minute TV program on WLMB, a local Christian television station in Toledo. The Lord gave me the name for the program: *Discovering the Jewish Jesus*. I filmed at WLMB's studio, and the program aired weekly. As a result of this outreach our congregation began to grow faster.

At the time, I had a lot of irons in the fire. I was pastoring Adat Adonai, I was speaking in other churches on Sunday mornings and/or evenings, and now I was filming the television broadcasts. Additionally I was still speaking to businesspeople during the week so I wasn't dependent on the congregation financially. This was very fortunate because with all the disagreements and animosity that had come with changing the trajectory of the congregation, the one thing I wasn't worried about was getting fired and losing my income from Adat Adonai. That was big. I think a lot of pastors make uncomfortable compromises and bad decisions when they are afraid of losing their jobs. I'm not accusing; I'm just telling the truth. The pressure is there.

In my case I wasn't afraid of losing my pastoring job because I had other income. I am thankful and fortunate that I did not have to contend with that issue; I was not depending on my rabbinate to support my family. So I just said what I thought needed to be said and did what I thought needed to be done without fearing the consequences. Again, as I look back, that was a huge blessing. It allowed me to preach the truth without fear.

Having had some success in the business world also helped in a number of other ways. Sometimes clergymen feel insecure because they wonder if they could cut it in the real world due to the fact that they often have never had a career outside fulltime ministry. But because I was able to gain the experience of being employed outside of ministry and achieving there, it increased my sense of competence and courage, allowing me to move forward with more forthrightness.

By this time, I was also carrying less religious baggage. One of my biggest prayers has been that the Lord would cleanse me of everything religious (everything born of manmade religion) that comes between me and Him. I want to be authentic and real. Don't you?

And I don't want my ministry to be a project but an overflow of my own quest for God.

As I have striven to live this way, the Lord has opened up many doors for me to share what I've experienced and learned. Much of what I teach has actually come from revelation and breakthroughs that God has personally led me into.

One instance that affected how I minister came in a dream while I slept in my office/bedroom in the Adat Adonai building. (I had a futon couch in my office that became my bed on Friday and Saturday nights.) In the dream I observed a game in which a circle of people were throwing a ball around to each other. There were maybe fifteen people in the circle. As I watched, the ball would come to one person, then that person would throw it to another person in the circle. I tried to discern if there was a pattern that governed the exchanges, but I couldn't see one. I stepped into the circle to play, and immediately the ball came to me. I didn't know what to do. I didn't know the rules. I didn't know what was going on. So I asked the person standing next to me in the circle, "What am I supposed to do with the ball?" The person just smiled and shook her head. Then I asked the man on the other side of me, and the same thing happened. I got so frustrated that I didn't know how to play and nobody would tell me what to do with the ball that I put the ball down and stormed away. I was frustrated and fuming.

Then the dream shifted, and I was now walking in a shopping mall filled with people. Along the way, I saw some people I knew, so I went up to them. I told them what happened in the circle and how mad I'd gotten when they wouldn't tell me how to play. The person I was explaining this to in my dream said, "Well, if you would have felt what was going on with the people in the rest of the circle, you would have known what to do with the ball."

As I puzzled over that, the Lord spoke to me (not audibly; I intuited it in my spirit), "You are performing. You're doing what you think you're supposed to do. You're preplanning too much of the services and are not sensitive to My Holy Spirit. You're ministering according to your own agenda. Whatever you've set in your mind beforehand to do, that's what you do. But that's not how the 'game' is played.

"When you get into the service, don't come into it with such a preconceived agenda. Be open and sensitive to My Spirit so you can discern and feel what I'm doing amongst the people, and then you'll know how to lead. You'll know what to do with 'the ball.'"

It was now obviously clear that God was telling me He wanted more control of our services. I just had to figure out how to be more sensitive to His Spirit's leading. It was something He would continue to teach me in the years to come. This revolutionized the way I ministered. We've had some pretty unique and powerful gatherings since then!

I began just waiting on God while ministering during services. I stayed in an active posture of trying to hear what the Holy Spirit was saying so He could direct me as to what to do next. Where previously I usually had a plan, now most days I have very little planned other than to let His Spirit lead me. I generally know what I'm going to preach on and from what part of the Bible, but largely I am just trusting the Lord to give me the thoughts and words to speak while I'm declaring His Word.

As I opened up to let God's Spirit lead me, we started as a congregation to experience the Holy Spirit's fellowship with us at a whole deeper level.

We were getting somewhere, but I had no idea the magnitude of where the Lord was about to take me.

19

GROWING IN SANCTIFICATION

BEFORE I COULD more fully enter into the next phase of ministry, God had a very personal breakthrough that I would need to have. Had I not broken through this, I don't think I would have ever been ready for the unpredictability of ministering in foreign lands—especially in developing countries.

Because I am such a high-voltage, driven person, it takes a lot to manage my emotions. Being high-voltage means I can get a lot done quickly, but it also means I can lack patience and become angry when something or someone gets in the way or slows me down. Perhaps you've had experience with people like that.

My anger would surface when Cynthia was running behind, causing me to be late for a meeting or an appointment. One time we had a really important meeting on a Thursday at 1:00 p.m., and I told Cynthia about it on Monday and let her know we couldn't be late. I reminded her again on Tuesday, and then again on Wednesday, trying to be really gentle about it but doing everything I could to be sure she would be ready when we had to leave on Thursday. "You know, honey, we really need to be on time for this meeting. It's going to be at 1:00 p.m., so we need to leave the house by 12:15 p.m. to get there on time."

Thursday came, and it was time to leave, so I called to Cynthia, "Honey, we've got to leave for that meeting in a few minutes."

"OK, I'll be right there!" she said.

So I went out, got in the car, and pulled it out of the garage.

And then I waited.

And waited.

The time came for us to leave. Then five more minutes passed. Then another five.

I started getting mad, then madder, and then madder still.

By the time we were close to fifteen minutes late, I was so enraged I felt like slamming on my car's accelerator and ramming right through our garage door. I mean, my anger was so over-the-top, I feel like I came very close to losing control and actually putting the car in gear, jamming my foot down on the gas pedal, and flooring it. I felt capable of driving my car right through my house, ending up with my house demolished behind me and my car sitting in the middle of my backyard.

Realizing how close I had come to doing this, I faced the fact that I had a problem, and it wasn't Cynthia. It was something in me.

Yes, the meeting was very important, and it would have been wise not to be late to it. I had the right to be angry but not like this. My anger was out of control.

Something in me needed to change. I couldn't put this all on Cynthia. I had a problem.

In that moment, the Holy Spirit spoke to me, saying, "You need to take responsibility for your own anger and stop blaming." Coming to grips with this brought a major shift in my life. It was a huge breakthrough.

That didn't mean controlling my anger got easier right away, though.

The first test came a week later. I was in Toledo to minister to our congregation on Saturday morning, and I'd been invited to preach later that afternoon at a big city outreach event downtown. I was bringing the dance team from our congregation to dance before I declared God's Word. Everything was set and planned out.

So again I said, "It's time to go, honey!"

She replied, "I'll be right there!"

And I went to the car and waited.

And waited.

I felt every second ticking by as I sat waiting in the car. Then Cynthia came. We were going to be late.

There I was driving on the way to preach, boiling with anger. It felt like every single cell in my body was crying out to scream at her. I was so frustrated and upset, but I knew what the Lord had told me. I had to take responsibility for my own anger and not blame it on Cynthia or anybody else.

It took every ounce of strength I had not to explode and scream at Cynthia for making me late again.

Somehow—I can't even explain it—but somehow, through resisting that anger when I felt like everything in me wanted to lash out, something changed in me. Somehow I got rewired on the inside. From then on it was much easier to control my anger. It's not that I didn't get angry anymore, but it was totally different after that. I could recognize the anger coming and then head it off before it got out of control. God supernaturally strengthened me through resisting.

This strength didn't just affect my new ability to manage my anger; it changed me in many ways. For example, if I came home after work and the house needed straightening up, rather than waiting for Cynthia to do it, I took initiative and began to help. (Cynthia was very busy also, so having her do everything was not right.) This shifting of perspective brought a major breakthrough in my walk with God.

This then led to another breakthrough for me—one that had been coming gradually over a long time and that transformed our marriage. If Cynthia and I were going to be used by God in a significant way, we needed revolutionary unity in our marriage. There is no covenant that sanctifies and creates spiritual power more than when God joins together a man and his wife to become one in Him and they do.

When Cynthia and I were first married, our having come from very different places, backgrounds, and cultures created a lot of stress and tension in our relationship. We were Jew and Gentile and had different personalities and very different temperaments. Differences often lead couples to hurt each other, and those hurts build up over time if they can't find a way to forgive and reconnect. We realized God had brought us together, but we had to die to ourselves to become one with each other.

The problem was probably more on my end because of my temperament. As I said, I run on a fast clock, I have a lot of drive, and I'm a fast talker. Cynthia, on the other hand, is more laid back and goes about life in a more even-tempered way. She's very precise, and sometimes I can be very impulsive because I want to just get things done. We sometimes see things differently and focus on different aspects of an issue. She's more relationally oriented while I am more goal focused. She's more of a detail person; I'm more big picture. In some ways Cynthia is more grounded while I at times can be more emotional and reactionary.

But over the years, Yeshua has changed us both for the better by imparting the best of each of us into the other. In other words, I am more patient and considerate due to Cynthia's patient nature being imparted into me, and Cynthia is more verbal and efficient due to my strengths being imparted into her.

The truth is without the love, wisdom, and healing that Yahweh imparted to me through Cynthia, I don't know where I would be today. The Lord has used Cynthia in my life to bring me into wholeness in a very deep and real way, and I am most indebted to her.

This breakthrough of being merged together so that the two became one in our relationship took place gradually and not without pain, but now Cynthia and I have a very blessed marriage. It has come through a process of being committed to God and to each other. We learned to love unconditionally and be sensitive to each other—as the Bible says, to esteem the other as higher than yourself (Philippians 2:3). In other words, we learned to put each other's needs first. Going from being far apart culturally and personality-wise at the beginning of our marriage to serving each other and becoming one flesh was a huge breakthrough. We're not perfect, but we're very blessed.

Over the years, Cynthia has matured into quite an effective tool in the Lord's hands. She is extremely compassionate and discerning of spirit. The Lord uses her to release His love and peace into His people's lives. It has been a fantastic blessing to be able to minister together. As I said, our marriage did not start out easy, but through perseverance we have been fused together by God to become a harmonious team, both relationally as a couple and in ministry.

Even with the healing in my marriage, I still craved more of God's peace in my life. I made it a focal point in my prayers. After I prayed for more of His peace for a year straight, Jesus again spoke to me through a dream. In the dream I found myself in the middle of an incredibly lush forest. It felt like it was somehow secret—like a secret forest that no one had ever been in before. All around the boundary there were these rock formations with ivy growing on them.

The forest was completely secluded and enclosed within these ivy-covered rock walls. The whole place was filled with peace and life. As I stood there in this luxurious, rich, green forest, I encountered the Spirit of the Lord. He started rolling over me in billows of heavy, powerful, thick peace. In all the prophetic dreams I'd had before, I'd just seen and heard what God was showing me; they were objective in nature. Truth was being revealed to me, but there was not much emotion involved. But this time, I fully felt waves and waves of indescribable, deep, deep peace both on me and inside me.

In the center of this forest there was a single wooden picnic table. There was nothing on the picnic table. I felt the Spirit of the Lord drawing me toward it. I knew that the peace was going to be even greater when I got there, as if the picnic table was a symbol of partaking of the Lord's peace and presence in the deepest and fullest way, but all of a sudden a scent came wafting toward me. It was the best-smelling pizza I'd ever smelled in my life, and it was less than an inch away from my nose! It was the most tantalizing thing I've ever smelled.

I became conflicted because on the one hand, I'd been praying for a year to have God's peace and now here it was, and if I yielded to the Spirit and simply walked deeper into the center of the forest toward that picnic table, I would experience even more. On the other hand, I'm smelling the most incredible pizza ever, and it made me ravenously hungry. I was torn in both directions. I desired more of God's shalom, yet my flesh was lusting for the pizza. Being conflicted, I compromised in my heart and reasoned, "Maybe I can have a bite of pizza and then yield back to the Spirit and go toward the picnic table." As soon as I entertained that thought and yielded to the possibility of pursuing that option, I woke up and the dream ended.

I got up out of bed and then sat on the couch in my bedroom, where I sometimes pray. I was so grieved. I asked God to forgive me for being willing to trade His peace for a lousy piece of pizza. I begged Him to let me go back to sleep, have the dream again, and give me another chance. I went back to bed, but the powerful outpouring of the peace of God did not return.

When I got up the next morning, I went back to my couch and prayed, "Lord, what happened? I've been praying for a year for peace, and You finally give it to me, and I traded it away for a piece of pizza? Even if it was the devil tempting me in the dream, I believe You were the architect of the dream. What are You saying to me?"

After much thought and prayer, I believed the Lord was telling me, "If you want more of My peace, you need to go on a fast." So for the first time in my life, I was able to go on a successful fast. I had tried many times before but had always broken the fast before I intended. What I decided to do was fast just one meal a day and then steadily increase the amount I was fasting over the next forty days. So the last three days I ate and drank nothing at all. I started getting painful muscle spasms in my feet and toes, and they began curling up on me because I had no potassium in my body. I didn't really have any great highs with the Lord during that time of fasting except for one intense moment when I had a very real sense that I was going to heaven. I still remember it.

I was a little disappointed at the end that I didn't have more sensational or spectacular experiences, but I believe what God was teaching me was that I needed to deny my flesh on a more regular basis. I needed to live a lifestyle of fasting. This included fasting by sitting and being still before the Lord. It also encompassed what I listened to, what I set my eyes on, the disciplining of my words—everything. Denying the flesh and being obedient to the Spirit is the way into peace. (See Galatians 6:7–9.) As we practice denying our flesh, subjecting our soulish impulses to the Lord and living in obedience to the Spirit, we find our way into peace. This visitation really marked me by helping me to more firmly grasp how important it is to resist and restrain our flesh. As we do, we will grow in power and be led victoriously from one breakthrough to the next.

Because I have shared several of my dreams, it's important for me to point out that I have been pursuing Jesus since 1978. These dreams didn't come all at once but were spread out over more than forty years of actively seeking Him. David said in Psalm 16:7, "I will bless the LORD who has counseled me; indeed, my mind instructs me in the night." I don't think it was anything I was doing that caused God to speak to me by His Spirit in my sleep. I think He has visited me in my dreams only because He loves me and desires to teach me. I know that I seem to have more revelatory dreams than many do; however, I also face more demonic activity at night in my sleep than most. We as the body of Messiah are in a war, and being on the front lines, I experience the battle intensely (Ephesians 6:10–17).

I don't look for the Lord to make Himself known only in my dreams; I also look for Him to be at work in my everyday life. Not long after *Discovering the Jewish Jesus* started airing in Toledo, I met Michael Hardy, who is now the chief operating officer (COO) of our ministry. He was a social worker, and he was counseling a young woman who was Jewish. He wanted to connect her with a faith community, and when he told her about Adat Adonai and she expressed interest, he got permission from the agency he was working for to bring her to one of our Shabbat services. He ended up falling in love with the teaching, so he started attending himself. We became friends, and we used to go out fishing once a year on the Sandusky River in Ohio. For us this basically amounted to fishing for catfish, as there's not much to catfishing. It's just a worm on a hook.

So there we were in this little boat, sitting a few feet apart. We'd put worms on our hooks and then drop them to the bottom of the river, where the catfish are. Over the next hour and a half I must have caught close to twenty catfish, and Michael had not caught one. We weren't doing anything different. We were sitting in the same spot and using the same bait, but I was catching fish and he wasn't. Something was strange. Suddenly the Spirit rose up inside me and I said, "Michael, grab your pole. You're going to catch a fish." Immediately he grabbed his fishing pole and as soon as he did, *bam!* There was the fish.

I knew when that happened that God was doing something and was uniquely involved in our relationship. It would be a few years before Michael came to work for me, but even before I hired him, Michael had a vision that God was about to do something big through *Discovering the Jewish Jesus*. Eventually I took a step of faith and asked Michael to come and work as our first full-time employee. We didn't have much cash on hand and didn't have much money coming in, so I told him that this was a faith venture. He didn't bat an eye. Today he supervises all our employees.

But more about the launch of *Discovering the Jewish Jesus* later. I'm a little ahead of myself.

20

IN HIS PRESENCE

A s the two most sacred Jewish holy days approached—Rosh Hashanah (the Jewish New Year) and Yom Kippur (the Day of Atonement)—I felt inspired to seek out and visit places where I had heard the Spirit of God was moving. I hoped I would receive something fresh from the Lord, a new impartation and revelation of His glory.

The first place I went was to a soaking conference in Toronto that was taking place in a church that some years earlier experienced a move of God that touched people's lives all over the world. Soaking involves just absorbing God's presence while being still and listening to very soothing worship music. Much of this soaking conference involved just sitting in God's presence as different anointed musicians played. I truly felt the Lord was drawing me into a deeper place through this practice of sitting in His presence and receiving, as Mary did when she sat at Yeshua's feet. (See Luke 10:38–42.)

Upon returning to Adat Adonai, I immediately instituted a time after our Shabbat service when we'd turn down the lights, play soft praise and worship music, and let people linger as late as they wanted to stay. It wasn't as if we suddenly had spectacular things happening in our midst because of this, but it seemed to soften the hearts of our congregation members and make them more sensitive to God's direction and Spirit in their lives. It definitely changed things for us, though it's hard to point to any specific results other than that the atmosphere of our gatherings and services transformed. People came more expectant of what God might do and teach them. There was also a more tangible or thicker sense of God's manifest presence in our midst.

Shortly after the soaking conference in Toronto, I went to visit the International House of Prayer of Kansas City, Missouri (IHOPKC). As soon as I walked into the IHOPKC prayer room, I experienced a marriage between what was going on in that room and my spirit, meaning I instantly felt connected. Twenty-four hours a day, seven days a week, musicians ministered unto God in the prayer room. The worship music was intermingled with prayers drawn straight from the Bible. For example, while the music was playing, the worship leader would literally sing a passage such as Ephesians 1:15–23:

> For this reason I too, having heard of the faith in the Lord Jesus which exists among you and your love for all the saints, do not cease giving thanks for you, while making mention of you in my prayers; that the God of our Lord Jesus Christ, the Father of glory, may give to you a spirit of wisdom and of revelation in the knowledge of Him. I pray that the eyes of your heart may be enlightened, so that you will know what is the hope of His calling, what are the riches of the glory of His inheritance in the saints, and what is the surpassing greatness of His power toward us who believe. These are in accordance with the working of the strength of His might which He brought about in Christ, when He raised Him from the dead and seated Him at His right hand in the heavenly places,

far above all rule and authority and power and dominion, and every name that is named, not only in this age but also in the one to come. And He put all things in subjection under His feet, and gave Him as head over all things to the church, which is His body, the fullness of Him who fills all in all.

The Scriptures were being sung twenty-four hours a day, seven days a week, as anointed worship teams (normally consisting of ten to twelve people) played their instruments and declared the Word of the Lord.

I'd never experienced anything like it. It was not religious. It was real. It was pure and authentic.

After spending five days there, I knew I had to bring this back to my congregation and establish a 24/7 prayer room in our building. The problem was, How were we going to man the prayer room twenty-four hours a day, seven days a week, when we had only about fifty people in our congregation? I knew that in order to successfully establish a 24/7 prayer room in our building, we would need a major and sacrificial commitment from all the members of our community.

In order to cast the vision, I decided to pay for everybody who was willing to visit the Kansas City prayer room. We had about thirty-five people who said yes. We paid for their hotel rooms, meals, and transportation. Our congregation left on a frigid day in December. The roads were so icy that only those who had to travel were out driving. Cars that had slid off the road were all over the place. I mean it was absolutely treacherous. But none of our members backed out, and everyone arrived safely—praise God!

Because we were going to need people to come into the prayer room at all hours of the night and day (usually people took between two- and eight-hour shifts), I knew I needed to expose them to the hardcore commitment and sacrifice this would involve. So once we were in Kansas City, I held mandatory prayer meetings at 3:30 in the morning. It was unbelievable! Everybody was in and excited.

Not long after we got back to Toledo, we launched our own prayer room that we call the Key of David. It began on Valentine's Day 2007, as we offered it up to Yeshua as a love gift. As of the writing of this book, we've had somebody in our prayer room twenty-four hours a day, seven days a week, for fourteen years. This is miraculous! Our congregation has experienced significant growth since then, but to consider that we launched it with fifty people is an outstanding mark and work of the Spirit.

I have discovered that by sitting before the Lord for significant lengths of time as we do in our prayer room, the Holy Spirit slowly draws us to and establishes us in Himself. This is how He responds when we do as His Word says—"Be still, and know that I am God" (Psalm 46:10, NKJV). As I practiced the spiritual discipline of sitting quietly before the Lord both in our prayer room at the congregation and the one Cynthia and I set up at home, the Spirit drew me out of being focused on the things that are outside of me and sensitized me in a much greater way to His presence inside me. Over time my life, as well as the lives of countless others, has been transformed by this practice. As we become more sensitive to the leadings, movement, and ways of the Holy Spirit by simply being still before Him, we're better able to abide in Him throughout our daily lives.

I cannot recommend this practice strongly enough. I encourage you to make a daily practice of just sitting before the Lord with gentle worship music playing. Look for songs that are not *about* God but are being sung *to* God. As I spent hours and hours in the prayer room, my personality began to change. Some people told me my voice didn't even sound the same. It got deeper and fuller. Even my next-door neighbor said, "You seem happier—like you're more at peace." One person said, "Rabbi, you're not even the same person anymore."

I made my life's priority in 2007–2008 to cease all unnecessary activity and instead just focus on and wait on God. I spent hour after hour, day after day, just listening to the sanctified worship music from IHOPKC that had the prayers and words of the Bible mixed in with it. My mindset was, "Lord, I am stopping my activity in the flesh to see You arise in my spirit." Sure enough, He did! After this time of doing nothing but waiting upon the Lord for a year, Jesus began to open bigger doors for me in ministry than I ever could have opened myself. I also began to see Yeshua working through me in the gifts of the Holy Spirit (namely discernment, prophecy, and healings) at a whole new level.

During this time, though I was maintaining my spiritual discipline of sitting before the Lord each day, there were times when it became difficult. God encouraged me through His Spirit in a dream. I was in a little one-room cabin. In the middle of the room was a simple wooden table, and on the other side of it sat a man whom I sensed was a familiar friend, but I didn't recognize Him. I also sensed I had been there for some time, and I was feeling antsy. I looked out the window of this cabin, saw the nature, and wanted to go out of the cabin and do something. I felt like, "I have been sitting here long enough. It's time for me to get out of here." I was on the edge of standing up and leaving when I heard a voice say, "That man sitting across from you who feels like a familiar friend is Jesus. Just keep sitting across from Him, and you'll be made whole."

What I believe the Lord was telling me was to continue to

practice sitting before Him in stillness. He was saying, "Don't run away when you get restless and uncomfortable or your mind tells you there is something else you should be doing. Believe in the process, even when it feels like nothing is happening and you're bored and fidgety. Continue to face Me and allow Me to bring to the surface what I need to heal so I can ground you in Myself and make you complete."

I felt the Lord was encouraging me to stay with the process and believe in it. I didn't need to be out in the world, talking to people, being busy, doing things—at least not for this season. Instead He was saying, "Just be still and focus on Me. I'm going to transform your soul and bring you shalom." (*Shalom*, as you may know, is the Hebrew word for peace and wholeness.)

I found myself walking that word out in a practical way that in the natural might have looked like a disaster. The building our congregation was meeting in had been sold, and we needed to be out of it in thirty days. We needed to find a new place to meet fast and preferably a building that we would own. Adat Adonai had never owned their own building in its seventeen years of existence. The Lord had changed me so much on the inside by waiting on Him, I decided I was going to wait on Him to provide us with our own building and not do anything about it until He told me to. I felt He instructed me to wait on Him for three weeks, and after I did so, He would either sovereignly bring a new building to us or supernaturally bless me after I had waited on Him to acquire a new building that He would lead us to.

I waited on Him for the complete three weeks, and at the end of that time we still had no building to move to and no leads for one. We now had only one week before we were to be out of the building we had been meeting in, but I was confident that because I had obeyed God, He would now bless my efforts and lead me to the right building. So the day after the three weeks of waiting were over, I got on the phone and called half a dozen realtors in our area to see what was available. None of them were in when I called, and none of them called me back that day.

I remember crying out to the Lord before I went to bed that night. "Lord, I trusted You in this. Now I've led my congregation off a cliff. What am I supposed to do now?" Truly I felt like the worst leader in the world. I felt like I had been totally irresponsible. "What kind of a rabbi," I asked myself, "would not have been thinking ahead and planning for this? You knew that you didn't own this building you are meeting in and eventually you would have to move out."

I was getting hit from the enemy on every side. (And understandably so, because in the natural my lack of planning had been irresponsible.)

Eventually I fell asleep. And as I slept, I had a dream. I saw a solid-gold spear that was about eighteen inches long, and it came and pierced through my forehead, right between my eyebrows. Then the Lord said, "You waited on Me till the end. You obeyed by trusting in Me and refusing to rely on your flesh. I've slayed you with My Spirit, and now you are going to be able to live in this reality of living by My Spirit rather than the flesh for the rest of your life."

As you've probably guessed, not long after that God brought us a building that we were able to buy, and we have never had to meet in somebody else's building since. Praise God! *Baruch HaShem!*

After we were established in our new building, I went to visit my mom, who wasn't doing well. My mom had developed diabetes in the mid-1990s, and it had grown gradually worse. Eventually my dad had to put her in a nursing home, as her health continued to deteriorate. Looking back, I wish I would have visited my mom more often. We were in Columbus, and she was in a Jewish nursing home called Menorah Park in Cleveland. On many of my visits I tried to share Jesus with her, but she never expressed any interest.

On this particular visit I had a supernatural sense of faith that she was going to receive the Lord that day. The four of us made the trip—Cynthia, our two daughters, and me. They'd put her in a wheelchair for our visit, so we went for a walk through the nursing home. When we'd come to a common area to sit with her for a bit, I asked, "Mom? If God would show you that Jesus is the Messiah, would you believe it?"

"I would," she said.

It was the most open I'd ever heard her. The four of us gathered closer around my mom, and I began to pray out loud. After a few minutes I asked her, "Mom? Are you feeling anything?"

"No," she said.

So we prayed again. I just knew that God was going to show up. After a little while more I said, "Mom? How about now? Do you feel anything?"

She looked at me. "Maybe a little," she said.

So we prayed again. I just had this confidence that the Spirit was going to break through and reveal Jesus as Messiah to my mother. "Mom, are you feeling anything now?"

"Yes," she said.

I said, "Mom, you said that if God would show you that what I'm sharing with you is true, that you would receive Yeshua. Do you want to do that?"

"Yes," she said.

So I led her in a salvation prayer, probably the most carefully articulated salvation prayer I have ever had anyone say after me. I covered every loophole I thought the devil might exploit, addressing everything I could think of from 360 degrees, making sure that every *i* was dotted and *t* crossed. While I know that salvation is more than just saying one prayer, I wasn't going to let this prayer with her be lacking in any way. What was amazing is that oftentimes my mother was not able to focus well because complications from the diabetes caused her to have mini strokes, which had damaged her mind. But during this prayer that she confessed back, she was totally clear and able to speak it out word for word.

We wheeled her back to the room and she said, "Who was that standing with us when we were praying?" There hadn't been anyone else with us, but I didn't say that. I just told her I didn't know. My daughter thought maybe her grandmother had seen an angel.

The next week or so I felt closer to my mom than I had in almost forty years. I felt such a deep love and connection with her like I did when I was a child.

I'd like to leave it at that because I believe her prayer was sincere, but that wouldn't be completely honest. After my mom prayed to receive the Lord, I felt such love for her. I would call her every day and try to build her up in the faith, but I could feel her faith wavering. A few weeks later she said, "I don't know if I believe in Jesus. I'm a Jew. I believe in Moses." She seemed confused. Not long after, she passed away. I am hoping God had mercy on her because she did open her heart to Him a few weeks earlier. I am hopeful that she is now in heaven.

Like Peter, who denied the Lord but because of God's grace was not ultimately lost, I am hoping that similarly the Lord honored my mother's prayer to receive Him despite her recanting when she was in a weakened state due to the fact that she was surrounded by traditional Jews who think believing in Jesus is anathema for a Jew. Seeing my mom in heaven would bring me joy deeper than my words could convey. I trust His grace. As for now, I am the only one in my family who believes.

I have very fond memories of my mother of blessed memory and know a lot of the reason for my success is because of her love for and belief in me. As a child I had a lot of confidence in my mom, which made me confident because I knew I was her son. I called her Mommy until I was around fourteen years old, and I only stopped because I didn't know anyone else my age who was still calling his or her mom Mommy. The confidence my mom had was imparted to me. Once Jesus healed me of the brokenness I described earlier in this book, it rose back up to the surface, and the Lord has used it for His purposes in my life.

About this time, an unexpected series of events led to something that would truly prove to be a breakthrough for our *Discovering the Jewish Jesus* telecasts. The president of WLMB, the Christian television station in Toledo we were broadcasting on, was also on the board of the National Religious Broadcasters, better known as the NRB. The NRB was given a channel on DirecTV because it was a public access channel. When they offered NRB the channel, the president of WLMB called me and said, "Listen, we were just given this channel on DirecTV, and we're looking for some original programming. Can we put *Discovering the Jewish Jesus* on the NRB Channel we're developing for DirecTV?" It was an easy decision. I told him, "Yes, thank you!"

Once we began airing on DirecTV, we went from a local station that was only broadcasting in Toledo to a national audience. It was a good place to start, but over time I felt like God had bigger plans for DJJ, but that involved us paying other stations to air our broadcasts.

A breakthrough came for us when a Jewish man in California saw *Discovering the Jewish Jesus* and had a very strong and distinct God encounter while watching the show. Somehow he tracked me down at Adat Adonai and reached out to tell me what had happened to him. He'd been searching for God for years, and when he watched our show, God confirmed to him that Jesus was the Messiah. "What can I do to help you?" he asked.

I told him about our wanting to take over the financial responsibility for airing our shows. The very next day, which just happened to be my birthday, I received a sizable check from him. Then a few months later he sent us another check that put *Discovering the Jewish Jesus* in a place where we could launch out. I put the money in the bank and waited on the Lord. Nine months later I asked the Lord if it was time to act and expand the broadcast, and I felt a confirmation in my spirit.

So we started shopping around for places where we could air *Discovering the Jewish Jesus*. Since that time, the Lord has opened doors for our broadcast all over the planet. And as a result people all over the world are being reached with Father God's love for them and the good news of Messiah Yeshua through television, radio, YouTube, podcasts, Roku, and now radio. Before I started in television, I had a dream in which T. D. Jakes laid hands on me as he was about to film for television and record for radio. When he laid his hands on me in the dream, I fell under the power of the Holy Spirit. I knew from this dream that God was calling me into television and radio. In 2021 we finally stepped out into radio, and I am currently on close to two hundred stations across the United States.

Yeshua inspired this Jewish man in California to give, and then He multiplied the man's offering as He did with the five loaves and two fish in Matthew 14:17–20. Now lives are being saved and changed every day as God's kingdom is being built through this ministry with the gracious help of our partners all over the earth.

21

TO THE ENDS OF THE EARTH

I N 2013 I got a call from a man in Haiti asking me to come and preach a crusade there. When I got that call, I knew I needed to answer yes.

Haiti became our first evangelistic outreach outside the United States. It was a life-changing experience. It was the first time I had ever encountered such strong demonic manifestations as I ministered.

I started by screaming at the demons as loud as I could. When I saw that was not effective, the Holy Spirit began to teach me. The Lord showed me that I didn't have to scream, that I already had authority. I discovered that when I look into the eyes of people who have demons and simply but firmly command the demons to leave in Jesus' name, almost always the demons disappear in a short period of time and the individual is then released in the love and peace of God right before my eyes. It is truly an amazing thing to witness people being set free in the name of Jesus.

Flying home from Haiti, I felt the depth and width of God's love as I remembered how thousands ran forward to receive

Jesus as their Messiah after I preached. I finally understood the next level of my calling in the Lord. I knew that God was now sending me to preach the gospel around the world through evangelistic outreaches. The only way I can explain how I felt about this is to say that I felt the powerful love of God for humanity and apprehended that He had called me to proclaim the good news of Christ Jesus to the nations.

After returning from that first trip, the Lord began to give me more and more insight about the spiritual warfare I had faced. One example of this came from a vision of the night. (See Acts 16:9.) In the dream I was living in a dilapidated house. The paint was chipping off; the yard was all weeds—the house was falling apart and badly broken down. As I looked out one of its windows, I saw a large, beautiful, brand-new home across the street. When I saw it, the Lord said, "That's your house."

I wondered, "If that's my home, why am I living here in this dilapidated house?" As I looked closer, I saw there were people in the new, beautiful home, and there was something strange about them. They had an intense, demonic energy about them. They looked like people, but they were energized with an intense hatred that I could easily tell was demonic. I was afraid of them. I realized the reason I was living in the deteriorated house rather than in the big, new, clean, contemporary home across the street that somehow belonged to me was that I was afraid to take possession of it. I was afraid of those demons that were living in it, and I was afraid to go over there and throw them out. Like the children of Israel who were afraid to take possession of the Promised Land because of the giants that were living in it, so too fear kept me from my promised land. (See Numbers 13:25–33.)

As the dream continued, I eventually got so sick and tired of living in the dilapidated home that I walked over to that new, clean house and stood outside the door, waiting for the squatter. There was a main guy, a head demon, and when he came out, I threw him on the ground and started wailing on him. I was punching as hard as I could, but my punches seemed to have no effect. But I had made up my mind, so I kept at it; I just kept on punching. I was not going to stop. Then suddenly—*poof!* It was like he'd been a balloon and I'd punctured him. He deflated and then disappeared.

I believe what the Lord was showing me is that He has an abundant life for us—beautiful, deep, rich experiences He wants us to have in Him. But we are not experiencing them because in order to enter in, we have to drive out the demonic forces that seek to intimidate us in order to prevent us from entering into our inheritance. Fear, the forces of darkness' chief tool, holds us back.

Fear is a prison. It keeps us in a dilapidated house.

The children of Israel thought themselves to be like grasshoppers before their enemy, but that was not who they really were. In God's reality they were the victors who could have driven the enemy out and taken possession of the Promised Land when He first sent them there. But they didn't. Instead they allowed the devil to twist and distort their thoughts because they didn't believe God and what He'd said they could do. (See Numbers 13:33–14:10.) What feelings of fear, inferiority, shame, and unworthiness are holding us back from entering into the fullness of our inheritance?

It's important for us to identify what is holding us back from living in the house God has for us. What's in the way that we need to evict? Unless we break through the fear and confront our wrong perceptions of reality and our demons, we won't experience the life God has planned for us in His Son.

I realized through this night vision that God had more for me and that there were things holding me back. I needed to be bold in confronting them and not give up, even when it felt like I was pounding against a brick wall that wasn't going to give. We often feel like we don't have power and that our efforts are not making a difference, but it's just the enemy deceiving us by trying to make us feel impotent, just as he did with Israel when they saw themselves as grasshoppers in the eyes of their enemy. In my dream, at first when I was punching the demon squatter, my punches seemed to have no effect on him. But the truth is, if we keep coming against what is holding us back—if we keep punching—we will break through by His strength and enter into more and more of God's fullness and freedom in our lives.

I'm aware of the warfare in the arena of my thoughts, and I struggle every day to break through—to break off evil, wrong attitudes, spiritual blindness, and ways of perceiving that are not of the Lord. For many of us the power of darkness has gained a foothold in our minds in relation to self-image. The first thing Adam and Eve experienced after they sinned was shame in relation to their bodies.

> Then the eyes of both of them were opened, and they knew that they were naked; and they sewed fig leaves together and made themselves loin coverings. They heard the sound of the LORD God walking in the garden in the cool of the day, and the man and his wife hid themselves from the presence of the LORD God among the trees of the garden. Then the LORD God called to the man, and said to him, "Where are you?" He said, "I heard the sound of You in the garden, and I was afraid because I was naked; so I hid myself."
>
> —GENESIS 3:7–10

Even as the children of Israel saw themselves as inferior (as grasshoppers) and believed the enemy saw them through that same lens, so many of us see ourselves as deficient and believe those around us see us the same way. Remember, the enemy seeks to steal, kill, and destroy, and we must confront his lies about God, ourselves, and the world around us. We can't be passive. We have to keep punching that demon until he finally disappears.

I want to see and think correctly. David said, "In Your light we see light" (Psalm 36:9). Through trusting and praying and crying out to God, I've slowly developed an internal power to break things off, rise up, be transformed, and see more clearly. *Baruch HaShem!* It doesn't always happen all at once. Usually it takes place little by little, as the Torah teaches.

> I will drive them out before you little by little, until you become fruitful and take possession of the land.
> —EXODUS 23:30

It's not that I've arrived, but I'm being changed. It's a journey through which we are going from strength to strength. (See Psalm 84:7.) One of my favorite Hebrew sayings is *Sheh Telchu MeKoach LeKoach* (May you go from strength to strength).

Again, in order for us to see rightly, we must fight, though many of us would prefer to avoid warfare. Yeshua Himself had to defeat the forces of darkness in the wilderness before He began to minster in the power of the Holy Spirit. (See Luke 4:1–14.) By facing and overcoming our challenges with the Lord's help, our spiritual strength is developed. It is actually part of the Lord's redemptive plan for us to have to warfare and fight in order to ascend in Him. Seven times in Revelation chapters 2 and 3 Jesus said, "He who overcomes," or "To him who overcomes." In

Revelation 3:21–22 Yeshua said, "He who overcomes, I will grant to him to sit down with Me on My throne, as I also overcame and sat down with My Father on His throne. He who has an ear, let him hear what the Spirit says to the churches." Let's stay encouraged because as we cling to Him, His power will be perfected in our weakness.

Depending on God as we war through all the battles we face in life is what makes us become strong in Him. When the apostle Paul was in the midst of tremendous spiritual warfare, he cried out to the Lord to deliver him from the battle. The Lord answered him by saying this: "My grace is sufficient for you, for power is perfected in weakness." Paul responded with these words: "Most gladly, therefore, I will rather boast about my weaknesses, so that the power of Christ may dwell in me" (2 Corinthians 12:9). The point is that engaging in spiritual warfare is a necessity if we are to grow up and become strong.

We can either put our heads in the sand and pretend everything is fine when it isn't, or we can rise up against the realm of darkness that is strategically targeting its energy against us, fight for our victory, become strong, and get breakthrough by the strength God will give us as we confront demons from the realm of darkness.

I remember an incident fifteen years ago. As I slept one night, I suddenly became intensely aware of the tremendous pain that was in my heart. It wasn't physical, but it hurt. It was a pain that I was not aware was there. It was as if the Lord tore away what normally prevented me from feeling the pain I was carrying and suddenly let me feel it all. In the midst of feeling this very severe pain, I heard an angel say, "You're on the right path."

You may ask me, "How did you know it was an angel?" I don't know how I knew—I just knew. The angel had the power to make me know he was an angel (although I can't say it was a "he." It wasn't like it had either a masculine or feminine personality. All I knew was that it was an angel.)

Then I said to the angel, "If I'm on the right path, why does it hurt so much?"

Then the angel said kindly back to me, "If you would cooperate more, it wouldn't hurt so much."

Then I said to the angel, "When will I be happy?" And this time, I heard not the angel but God's Spirit speak back to me, "When you get strong, you will be happy."

The longer we war, the more strength we gain, and as we gain strength, we'll be able to rise up and confront the darkness that is keeping us bound. In my experience the hardest thing about overcoming darkness is facing the darkness in the first place. Once we face the darkness, the darkness breaks—it has to. As soon as it is confronted by the spirit of light, it instantly breaks. The hard part is gathering the strength to start setting our faces against it. It's not something that happens all at once. It's an everyday struggle. We must keep pressing in, and little by little we get stronger and break through into the light, where God's fullness is realized.

As Father continued to train me in spiritual warfare, He also continued to open doors. In 2014 we returned to Haiti to speak in two locations, and then we were in Kenya, Tanzania, and Uganda, speaking in eight different cities. In Haiti we saw hundreds of salvations, deliverances, and healings, including a woman who had been the queen of a voodoo parade in the city we were in, Saint-Marc. She came up to the platform and publicly told all who were present that she was giving up voodoo, that it hadn't satisfied her, and she was giving her life to Jesus.

We saw extreme demonic manifestations and deliverances as

I preached the gospel, no different from what you'd read about in the Bible. The most touching one was of a young girl, about seven years old, who started rolling around on the ground. Her eyes tilted and rolled back in her head, as she was utterly captive to the powers of darkness. After I commanded Satan to loose her and told the demon to leave, she became like a different person. In an instant her eyes cleared and were washed of the terror, confusion, and evil that had bound her. They turned into beautiful little girl's eyes in which you could see the beauty and love of God. Tears started streaming down her cheeks. She was delivered! When I saw the response and miracles taking place as I preached the gospel, I finally understood what God had meant when He told me, "You are an evangelist," all those years ago.

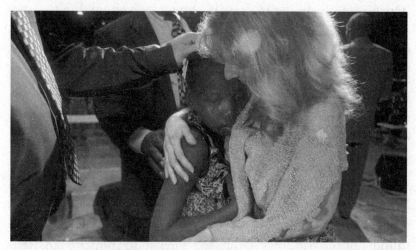

Cynthia hugs the young girl who was set free from the powers of darkness. After we prayed for her, she became like a different person.

The first place we went in Kenya was Kakuma, one of the largest refugee camps in the world. Kakuma means "nowhere" in Swahili.[1] It is located in the northwestern region of Kenya and is literally in the middle of nowhere. There is only one road in from the remote location where our plane had landed, and the road had so many potholes—some at least two feet deep—that we literally had to drive off the road as much as on the road as we traveled for what seemed like forever.

We arrived at Kakuma late at night, so I couldn't see much at all, but when I got up the next morning, walked outside, and saw all the people hoping to get into the refugee camp—people from Sudan, Ethiopia, and Somalia—I was blown away. It was like I was transported thousands of years back in time as I saw these isolated and primitive beloved souls dressed the same way they have for countless centuries.

In addition to all the nationalities that populated the refugee camp were the indigenous people of that region called the Turkana, who are one of the oldest civilizations on earth. They lead a hard life, living in thatched huts made by mixing together sticks and whatever else they can find to build them. But the biggest problem is that Kakuma is in a desert-like region where there is no water. The indigenous people had to dig down into the ground for drinking water. They would even come out of the desert to stand by the road with small water bottles hoping a car would stop and pour some water into their bottles.

One day my team took a Jeep ride with our Kenyan coordinator deep into the desert where the Turkana were living. I mean there was nothing but desert: no roads, utilities—nothing. It definitely felt like we were in the middle of nowhere (*kakuma*). As I looked out the windows of the Jeep, I began to think, "Man, what happens if we break down out here?" I voiced my concerns to our Kenyan bishop. He boldly replied, "Fear is never wise." I've never forgotten those words of wisdom.

I was blown away by the whole experience!

This first crusade in Africa was very small, a few hundred

people. But over the years they have kept growing and growing, with our largest crowds estimated by various sources at between 50,000 and 100,000. (See picture of crowd size in photo section.)

In 2015 we were back to Kenya and Uganda, as well as doing mass evangelistic outreaches in Zambia and Malawi. In Kalulushi, Zambia, after I declared healing into the lives of those present, we had a fifteen-year-old boy who, according to his sister who came up to the platform to testify with him, hadn't talked since he was born. The young boy stood next to his sister with the microphone to his mouth saying slurred words for the first time in his whole life. His sister told the crowd, "I thought this kind of stuff only happens on TV. Now I have seen it for myself."

We've seen many healings and deliverances over the years. One that really touched me that I believe is genuine but can't prove was when a young boy who was about eleven or twelve years of age came forward. He had been unable to learn to read, but he stood and faced the crowd who had gathered and said, "God told me I'm going to be able to learn to read now." I believed him and was very moved. Generally, when children testify, I believe them.

The climax of this evangelistic outreach in Zambia was when a Baptist pastor who had been taught not to believe in the gifts of the Spirit was with me on the platform and a man began to manifest a demon. They brought the man up to the platform, and I turned and said to the Baptist pastor, "Cast it out." He looked at me with eyes as big as saucers. I told him again, "Cast out that demon." He had observed me doing it for three days. So he, with fear and trepidation, walked over to the man and commanded the demon to leave. It did. That Baptist pastor was ecstatic—probably much like Jesus' disciples were in Luke 10:17–20 after they had cast out their first demons. By the time I left, that Baptist pastor was an altered man. He had entered into the supernatural realm of the Holy Spirit.

Another unique memory from the mission field is when my executive producer, Dustin Roberts, had a dream that we were going to be ministering to prostitutes. We had never done so before, but sure enough a day or two after his dream, one of the pastors approached us and said he had a ministry specifically to prostitutes. Because of the poverty, many young women had resorted to selling their bodies just to have enough money to survive, and they often didn't see any other way to make it. He asked me if I'd be willing to minister to these prostitutes he was trying to reach. Obviously I said yes, and my team and I were then taken to a building where he had gathered about fifteen young women. They were there because they wanted to be free but had not yet been successful in breaking away from the lifestyle they were trapped in. About half of them gave their lives to the Lord during this time of ministry. Several years later the pastor reported to us that the women were still walking in freedom and planted in local churches.

At every international evangelistic outreach my team and I have done, in addition to the masses who respond to the invitation to ask Jesus to forgive and save them, we have seen many souls come forward with testimonies of being bodily healed. "And they went out and preached everywhere, while the Lord worked with them, and confirmed the word by the signs that followed" (Mark 16:20). My evangelistic outreaches involve preaching the gospel (the good news of Messiah Jesus), healing the sick, and casting out demons. We believe this is the biblical model. Everywhere Yeshua went, He preached the gospel, healed the sick, and cast out demons. This is also the pattern of ministry that Yeshua gave to His disciples.

And He called the twelve together, and gave them power and authority over all the demons and to heal diseases. And He sent them out to proclaim the kingdom of God and to perform healing.

—LUKE 9:1–2

The practical struggle I was having on the mission field was knowing how to respond to many of those who were testifying of being healed. Some came forward and said, "I had a headache for two days, and now it's gone." The crowd would go wild, but I was skeptical. I'd be thinking, "That's good, but was that really a miracle?" I mean a lot of people get headaches that go away in a few days. Others would come and say they couldn't walk before without using their stick or cane, but now they claimed to be healed. We'd ask them to show us, and they would hobble across the platform, and the crowd and the ministers on the stage would be shouting and jumping up and down with excitement, but I was not convinced. I thought, "I don't know. There's a lot of adrenaline here right now. This man is still limping a lot. It may just be the adrenaline in his system that's energizing him to walk without his stick right now."

Others came up and testified to being healed, but I questioned if they'd come up to testify in front of the crowd just because they craved attention and wanted to be seen by everybody. (Sorry for being such a skeptic, but I didn't want to act like God had just done a miracle when I wasn't fully convinced that He had. When I interviewed those who were claiming to be healed, I asked hard questions to try to verify if they were authentic healings.) Some of the native pastors began to admonish me not to be skeptical but to celebrate the miracles. I couldn't do it. I celebrated when I thought something was genuine, but oftentimes I remained unconvinced that a bona fide miracle had just taken place, so I simply said, "Praise God," and moved on to the next testimony.

I began to pray, "Father, show me a miracle that is undeniable!" And then it happened.

In Lira, Uganda, we were holding a mass evangelistic outreach for four days from Thursday to Sunday night, and a woman who was totally and legally blind had been brought to our crusade. She believed the Lord was going to heal her. I had no idea who she was or that she was there. She came for the first night on Thursday, but nothing happened. The friend that took her to the grounds where our outreach was being held said to her when he dropped her off, "Woman, what are you going to do? You can't even see."

She replied, "God is going to heal me."

Nothing happened Friday night or Saturday night, but she testified on film later that since she *knew* she was going to be healed, she was not discouraged. On Sunday night for our last meeting, there were thirty thousand Ugandans present. The meeting had been going on with praise and worship along with special guest musicians and dancers for about three hours before I took the platform. By the time I got up, it was getting dark. I preached the Word and declared the Lordship of Messiah Jesus, and then I began to declare healing over the massive sea of souls. Under the unction of God's Spirit I said forcefully and with great authority, "Blind eyes, be opened!" As I commanded, "Blind eyes, be open!" a lightning bolt flashed in the sky. (We have it on film!)

After I got done commanding and releasing the healing power of God over the crowd, we asked for testimonies. I explained that some healings happen instantaneously, others happen over time, and others, for reasons we don't understand, don't occur until we see Jesus face to face. What we do know is that by His stripes and wounds, we are healed. (See 1 Peter 2:24.) As Matthew recorded, "He Himself...carried away our diseases" (8:17).

People began to come forward to share with the crowd what God had done for them. We had many of the usual testimonies. People claiming they could now hear well, people being able to move their arms and their head when they had no ability previously, headaches leaving, no more abdominal pain, and so on. Then this woman was escorted to me as I stood in the center of the platform. She had been blind but had suddenly started to see. One of the pastors put her in front of me. I continued to release healing, and then all the sudden she was completely healed! We have the testimony of her daughter, the manager at the hotel that she used to sit in front of to beg, and of countless others that knew her before she was healed, all testifying to the authenticity of this miracle. My team went and interviewed the witnesses. You can view it on YouTube if you search for "Rabbi Schneider Blind Woman Sees After 15 Years...Miraculously Healed."[2] (There are several videos on this, make sure to watch the one that is 6:51 in length.)

God had answered my prayer. He had done an extraordinary miracle that I was convinced was authentic. This put a lot of wind in my sails to continue to boldly proclaim not only salvation but healing in the one and only name of Yeshua the Messiah, confident that people would be bodily healed as I did.

CONTINUING TO BREAKTHROUGH

I WAS GROWING EXHAUSTED in the midst of traveling back and forth to Africa and overseeing our congregation, whose name we had changed to Lion of Judah to reach more people beyond the Messianic community. Cynthia and I found we needed to take more time to recharge. We started going to a small, secluded cabin deep in the Rocky Mountains of Colorado, where we are surrounded completely by huge evergreens. We go there to just be alone with the Lord in nature, like Jesus, who often went up into the mountains to pray with His Father in a lonely place. (See Matthew 14:23 and Luke 6:12.)

One night while I was there on one of our visits, the Lord spoke audibly to me as I was lying in bed with Cynthia and clearly said, "Your *only* gift is breakthrough." One would think I would have been elated that Father had spoken to me, but in reality it hurt my feelings. The next day I walked around mulling it over. "What does this mean, Lord? Does this mean I'm not a good preacher? Does it mean I'm really not a gifted teacher? Is my only gift to be the first one through the wall?"

As I prayed about it more and more, I came to understand that the Lord was saying, "I'm not telling you that you're not an anointed preacher. I'm not telling you you're not an anointed teacher. You are, but I have many people who are anointed preachers and teachers. But the gift I've given you that is distinct and that few people have is the gift of breakthrough."

God has called me to be a pioneer and a forerunner. I know that there have been other Jewish ministries on television. However, I was the first one to come out every week preaching the Word of God dressed like a Jew, wearing my yarmulke and prayer shawl and now my *peyos* (sidelocks), and using a preaching-teaching format instead of an interview-guest format. Another feature that makes *Discovering the Jewish Jesus* unique is that I'm not just focusing on Israel or Jewish themes, but I'm teaching to the best of my ability the whole counsel of God. I don't fit in the mold of either the traditional Gentile church or the mainstream Messianic movement.

Being the first one to do something often comes with rejection by the old guard who have always done things a certain way, and I have certainly experienced my share of rejection. When someone is the first one to break through the wall, he will always get bloodied. I am actually thankful for the rejection I have received, because it forces me to cling to Father and Messiah Jesus even more tightly. By being on the outside, Father can speak to me and direct me in ways that I wouldn't be open to if I were one of the good ole boys and too concerned about fitting in with the group. It can be lonely at times, but I feel blessed to be a forerunner and wouldn't want it any other way.

I often sense God's presence most keenly in nature. Whenever Cynthia and I can get away to Colorado, I enjoy going fishing. In this photo, I caught a trout.

Spending time deep in the Colorado mountains could not last forever. We had more work to do. In 2016 we had outreaches in ten cities in Brazil, Uganda, and Cuba. Cuba had been a closed country and had just opened its doors, enabling my team and me to come and preach the gospel, but we had to be very careful about what we said, because we were told that there were government spies all over. Cuba's government consists of one party.

It is a Marxist-Leninist socialist state. Freedom of religion is still sometimes suppressed.

They were in the midst of revival in many places in Cuba, and we experienced this in the local congregations where we ministered. Due to the strict controls of the state, we were not permitted to do our usual, large outdoor outreaches but were restricted to meet inside local churches. Because Cuba is a land that has been heavily influenced by witchcraft, we saw some strong deliverances taking place as the truth of Jesus was forcefully proclaimed.

But the most incredible deliverance scene that I've ever witnessed happened when we were in Gulu, Uganda. Gulu was a stronghold of Joseph Kony of the Lord's Resistance Army (LRA), a terrorist group that violently murdered thousands of people and abducted at least twenty-five thousand children over the years of its existence.[1] Kony held the city captive, kidnapping many children from their villages and making them soldiers in his cult. The war between the Ugandan government and Kony's army was so severe that in 1996, the government ordered all citizens in northern Uganda (Kony's stronghold area) to relocate to internally displaced person camps, which at the time had an estimated population of two million people in them.

By 2007 Kony's forces had been driven out, but when we were there, the city of Gulu was still recovering and in need of healing from the trauma. I was told that everybody in the area had been affected and knew people who had been killed there during the war with the Lord's Resistance Army (a name that is utterly twisted and deceiving since they relied on witchcraft).

One morning my team and I were having breakfast outside at our hotel in Gulu, and an American young woman of about twenty-five years of age approached our table and asked if she could sit with us. We were the only Americans at the hotel. "Sure," I said. "Sit down."

We began to talk, and she asked us what we were doing there. I explained that I was an evangelist and that we had come to preach the good news of Messiah Jesus. She responded, "I don't believe in God. I'm a scientist." (She was there doing some type of medical testing.)

"That's a problem," I said to her. "Where do you get consciousness from? Where does the ability to love come from?" Then I pointed to a beautiful red flower behind her. "Where does beauty come from?" She then asked where our meeting was going to be that night, and I told her. Sure enough she came. She was towards the front of a crowd of about thirty thousand people. She wasn't hard to see because she was Caucasian and there were no more than a handful of Caucasians present. I had one of my team members bring her to the podium where she stood off to the side. I wanted her to see with her own eyes some of the miracles God was doing.

As I began to declare the Word of God, people started shrieking, as many demons were manifesting. I motioned to the local ministers to bring one woman up to the platform whom the powers of darkness were loudly, wildly, and violently manifesting through. When the ministers placed the woman on the platform, I began commanding the devil to let her go, taking authority over the demons that were manifesting through her. When I spoke into the microphone so everybody could hear and commanded Satan to release her, suddenly demons started manifesting in over a hundred people in the crowd. People young and old, male and female, started shrieking, falling, convulsing, flailing, kicking, punching, and foaming at the mouth. It was pandemonium.

I felt like we were on the verge of mass hysteria and that the platform might be overrun, but demons were leaving. One of our team members who was a native Ugandan said, "The demons are popping out like popcorn!" People were being set free. I felt like I was in the Book of Acts. It was unbelievable and surreal. The bottom line is that mass deliverance took place that night. Because these residents had been through such trauma due to the war with Joseph Kony and the LRA and because ancestral religion and witchcraft had been so much a part of their culture, many demons had gained entrance but had now been exposed.

The next morning, my team and I were again outside at our hotel for breakfast. The young scientist who had observed all this came up to me as I was standing in line to get some food. "Thank you," she said to me. "I'm going home this afternoon. Thank you for your wisdom." She had become convinced. God proved to her that He was real and His love for people was powerful and authentic.

In 2017 we traveled for evangelistic outreaches to Uganda, Kenya, Brazil, Nigeria, and Israel. In Jerusalem we held an event that drew about five hundred Jewish people who had made *aliyah* (immigration of Jews to Israel) from the former Soviet Union and who did not have a personal relationship with Yeshua. We partnered with a Messianic ministry there to provide them humanitarian aid, as well as to present the good news of Yeshua to these Russian-speaking Israeli Jews.

As I got up to preach, I felt an unction. I mean I knew I was anointed by the power of the Spirit, but the people sat there expressionless. I didn't know if one word I said was penetrating, but I knew I was proclaiming Messiah in the power of the *Ruach HaKodesh* (Holy Spirit). I was getting to the end of my message. I started giving my call for people to respond. They looked as hard as stone. Then I saw it—a tear was streaming down a young woman's face in the first row. She was gently shaking. She raised her hand. She wanted to receive Yeshua. Then another hand went up, then another. We had well over a hundred Jewish souls raise their hands. Then they stood and prayed to receive Messiah Yeshua as their Savior. It was one of the most beautiful days in my ministry.

That same year, we also went to preach Messiah Jesus in Nigeria for the first time. The Nigerians were much more intense, energetic, and aggressive than the Africans I had met in the other countries where I had been. This outreach in Nigeria came about when a fairly well-known Nigerian gospel singer sought me out in order to bring me to Nigeria. He felt his people needed to hear a deeper truth. He was concerned that too much of the Christian culture in his country was seeking God for His blessings but not really seeking God for Himself. He felt that the Lord was telling him, "Bring Rabbi to Nigeria." With his help we were able to put together a very large evangelistic outreach in Enugu, Nigeria, where tens of thousands of people went forward and prayed to receive the Lord. That was the first of several other large evangelistic crusades we did in that country.

Some parts of Nigeria are very dangerous, and my team and I are always accompanied by security when traveling. I remember the first time I was being driven by armed security people from Lagos, where the airport is, to Enugu, where our outreach was. As we started getting deeper into Nigeria's interior, there were many military people standing in the middle of the streets. After observing this for a while, I said to my armed security guard in the front passenger seat, "Why are these military personnel lined in the middle of the streets with their rifles?" He said, "To prevent people from being kidnapped while they're driving down the road." The bandits would hide in the thick weeds on the side of the road and then ambush cars and kidnap people for ransom. We had to be very careful while there. Michael Hardy, our COO, works very hard to keep us safe.

One funny incident (not at the time but looking back) that happened in Nigeria is when a governor of a city we were ministering in offered to let my team and me stay in the governmental State House. It looked really impressive, and Michael was delirious with delight when the governor offered it to him on his pre-visit. (Michael travels to wherever I will be ministering in advance to get everything in order.) Michael called me from Nigeria, "Rabbi, this is awesome! The governor has offered for us to stay in the governmental State House." He sent me pictures. The rooms were huge and very presidential looking. This was the last Michael talked to me about it for a few months.

Then a few days before the outreach, Michael said to me, "Ah, Rabbi, just to give you an advance warning, the beds are not like here; they're harder. You may want to bring an extra blanket to lay on the bed."

"How hard are they, Michael?" I asked.

"Pretty much like sleeping on the floor."

I went out and bought an air mattress that I brought with me, but the story was far from over. In the airport in Amsterdam, halfway there, Michael said to me a little sheepishly, "Oh, Rabbi, you may not want to leave any cookies or any of your food uncovered. I recommend putting everything in Tupperware containers."

"Why?" I said.

"When I was there last time, I saw a rat in my room," Michael answered.

It was a lot for this Jewish boy to get his head wrapped around! But we look back and laugh about it now.

Before COVID-19 shut travel down in 2020, I had spoken in Africa twenty-eight different times in twenty-five different cities in the nations of Kenya, Uganda, Zambia, Malawi, Tanzania, Nigeria, and Ghana.

Being in these places reconnected me with my boyhood sense of wonder at the grandeur of God in nature and creation. On one of our trips to Kenya we saw all kinds of animals: lions, leopards, zebras, rhinos, giraffes, and a variety of antelope—quite an adventure. Believe it or not, though, even more striking to me than all the animals was seeing the night sky deep inside Kenya without any cities or nearby lights to compete with it. In that immense African sky it seemed like the stars were so close. I remember just lying outside on my back by myself, looking up at the stars. They were so impregnated with the glory of God. It was spectacularly powerful and beautiful.

Although corruption is rampant in some places in Africa, for the most part the peoples of Africa are precious. There is an innocence, a humility, a faith, and a desire to receive that I have not found anywhere else. When Jews who believe in Jesus, like myself, come to Africa, it's like their level of faith goes through the roof. They say things like, "If a Jew is coming to preach Jesus to us, Jesus must be getting ready to come back soon." They know that my coming to them is prophecy being fulfilled: "In those days ten men from all the nations will grasp the garment of a Jew, saying, 'Let us go with you, for we have heard that God is with you'" (Zechariah 8:23).

Because of this we have great favor from the Lord in Africa. Over the years, we have met with and ministered to kings, governors, the parliament of Uganda, and the man who is now the president of Malawi. When we arrive, we are often taken in at the airport through a VIP entrance. They value men and women of God in a way the United States does not. Africans' view of the US is that because our country was founded on God, America became great. Unfortunately it seems that in some ways, now African leaders are seeking to found their countries on God and America has fallen away. Everywhere in Africa they bring God into their lives. They name their businesses, their children, and even their busses after God. There are hotels called El Shaddai, children named Innocent, busses with a banner declaring Jesus is Lord running down the side.

Me with the king of Cape Coast, Ghana, shown wearing the prayer shawl I gave him

Sometimes upon arrival the first place we've gone is to meet the ancestral king of the province we are ministering in. The most memorable time was with the king of Cape Coast, Ghana. It was a lot like you think it would be. It was surreal. We drove to the king's palace. When we arrived, about a dozen women dressed in their colorful ancestral clothes encircled us and started dancing a traditional African dance. Next we were escorted in to see the king, who was dressed in his ancestral royal garb and had his staff in hand. He was very warm. He attended every night of our outdoor outreach to hear the gospel being preached with signs and wonders following.

I even had one very high-ranking political leader contribute financially to the ministry because he was so convinced it was of God and wanted to be part of it. (It should be noted that we never charge any money to the local churches to come, nor do we take offerings for our ministry while there. *Discovering the Jewish Jesus* pays for all our outreaches, and those that are financially supporting this ministry are the real heroes. It is because of them that hundreds of thousands of Africans have been touched by the love of King Jesus.)

We are also continuing strong outreach in Israel through television, a special YouTube channel where my programs are translated into Hebrew, and on-the-ground ministry there. On our last trip to Israel I ministered to Holocaust survivors. I was very nervous about going to minister to these Holocaust survivors and had to be very careful about the way I delivered my message. I shared the testimony of how I as a Jew came to faith in Yeshua and that the God of Israel, who appeared at Mount Sinai, is alive and loves us today. One man stood up and objected, but most listened, and some of them prayed to receive Yeshua as their Messiah after I delivered God's Word. We were told that it was a groundbreaking event.

Because of the persecution from the Orthodox that Messianic Jews in Israel have often received, many Messianic Jews there have reacted so strongly against traditional Orthodox Judaism that they, in my opinion, at times throw the baby out with the bathwater. I personally, however, want to glean from Judaism the riches that are there.

> And Jesus said to them, "Therefore every scribe who has become a disciple of the kingdom of heaven is like a head of a household, who brings out of his treasure things new and old."
> —MATTHEW 13:52

I respect my heritage and want to receive the anointing that is upon it. My ancestors met God in His power and glory 3,500 years ago at Mount Sinai. I believe there is still a residue of that anointing upon God-fearing religious Jews today that I want to absorb. Absolutely they cannot get to heaven without Yeshua, but some carry the anointing of the fear of God: "The fear of the LORD is the beginning of wisdom" (Proverbs 9:10).

There is no question that there are many traditions of men within rabbinic Orthodox Judaism that need to be rejected. (See Mark 7:7–8.) Yeshua also taught, however, that "salvation is from the Jews" (John 4:22) and that teachers who help God's people understand the Torah through the lens of the New Testament would be "called great in the kingdom of heaven" (Matthew 5:19). My point is that as a Messianic Jew who also shows respect for my religious heritage, I am at times standing alone.

Not too long ago I walked into the administrative office of one of the most well-known congregations in Jerusalem. When I walked in, the secretary recognized me. "Rabbi Schneider!" she said excitedly. "I have been watching you on television for a few years, and it is so refreshing to see a Messianic Jew dressing like a Jew and wearing a *kippah* [the Jewish skullcap also called a yarmulke]." As a Messianic Jew she wanted to still feel Jewish, and my presence helped her to do that.

When I show up in the congregations where I am invited

to deliver God's Word wearing my *kippah* and prayer shawl, it seems to affirm them in their Jewishness. They are surrounded in Israel by millions of Jews who don't believe in Jesus and say you can't remain Jewish and believe in Jesus. When I arrive dressed like a Jew, they are affirmed with the truth, "Yes, you can be a Jew and believe in Jesus, and in fact, these are the truest Jews of all."

So far the place my ministry has had the greatest reception in Israel is among the Messianic congregations that are made up of Jews who moved to Israel from the former Soviet Union. We hope to see our outreaches in Israel and around the world continue to grow in the days ahead.

TRANSFORMATIONAL REALITIES

A s I LOOK back over my life and seek to understand how I got to where I am today and how breakthroughs have happened, certain elements stand out. I share them with you in hopes you might be able to apply them to your own life.

1. Believe it all begins and ends with the grace of God.

He is the author and finisher of our faith. We must cast our entire existence into His hands and realize that at the end of the day, everything good that happens to us is a gift from Him.

2. Have a vision for more of God.

Jesus said, "So if the Son makes you free, you will be free indeed" (John 8:36). Imagine what it would feel like to be totally free—free of worry, fear, and all bondage.

I'm talking about spiritual breakthrough. We must have vision for and believe that breakthrough into freedom by God's Spirit is possible. No matter where you are right now, God will bring His own into victory. "Is anything too difficult for the LORD?" (Genesis 18:14).

3. **Have childlike faith.**

Over the years, I see that I had a simple, childlike faith. I believed God loved me, so I was not afraid to take risks.

4. **Be willing to be different and pay the price.**

How can we have breakthrough if we just want to fit in? If we are just like everybody else, we won't get breakthrough. Yeshua said, "How can you believe, when you receive glory from one another and you do not seek the glory that is from the one and only God?" (John 5:44). In other words, if we are more concerned about fitting into the crowd and being liked and accepted than we are about getting free, we will never get breakthrough. We have to step out. Trust Yeshua and follow Him, even if it means being misunderstood or rejected by family, friends, and those around us. Forerunners, pioneers, and those who get breakthrough are not controlled by wanting to be liked by others. And remember, the first one through the wall will always get bloody. There is a price to pay for breakthrough.

5. **Take action.**

My dad said to me one time, "Keep shaking the bushes and eventually something will fall out." There is a time to act. Jesus said to the man with the withered hand, "'Stretch out your hand!' He stretched it out, and it was restored" (Matthew 12:13). This man wasn't healed until he did something. We have to participate with God in order to get breakthrough. After King David defeated his enemies, he declared, "God has broken through my enemies *by my hand*, like the breakthrough of waters" (1 Chronicles 14:11, emphasis added).

Notice God broke through by David's hand. The Lord said to Moses when the children of Israel needed a breakthrough in order to be saved from the Egyptians, "Why are you crying out to Me? Tell the sons of Israel to go forward. As for you, lift up your staff and stretch out your hand over the sea and divide it, and the sons of Israel shall go through the midst of the sea on dry land" (Exodus 14:15–16). Moses and Israel had to act to see God's power released—don't hesitate to take action when the Holy Spirit is leading you to act.

6. **Expect opposition.**

Supernatural anointings attract supernatural opposition. Consider the fate of John the Baptist and the twelve apostles. Consider also that Yeshua said, "If they persecuted Me, they will also persecute you" (John 15:20). Expect resistance. Breakthrough requires that you press through resistance without giving up.

7. **Cling to God.**

Some years ago I had taken a team to minister to a church on a Sunday night. It was a team from the Messianic congregation I was shepherding, and I brought our dance troupe with me. It was a very frigid winter night. At the end of our ministry, at about nine o'clock at night, everyone was leaving the sanctuary, including my dance troupe. All of a sudden (I was still in the building packing up all my things) the husband of one of our dancers ran into the building from the parking lot in a panic. He said, "Come and help! My wife just fell down in the parking lot!" (The parking lot was extremely icy from the cold.)

His wife was a thin, frail woman of about sixty. Without another thought I looked up and asked, "Lord, why did this happen? This woman just got done dancing for You. Surely You could have kept her from falling! I am having a hard time believing this is part of Your will for her. I would think You would have had

197

something good in store for her as a result of her devotion and dancing tonight. I don't understand it. I can't bury my head in the sand about this. I've seen too many believers who claim to know You but live in a constant state of failure and defeat. Your Word says that You protect us, will bless us, and give us victory. This doesn't line up with Your Word. Until I have an answer, I don't know if I can go on." It wasn't that I was giving up my faith, but I did need an answer.

Two days later the Holy Spirit clearly spoke to me as I was driving in my van. "The reason you see My people falling and failing," He said, "is because they are not trusting Me."

When He said the word *trust*, beloved one, it was filled with revelation—I understood exactly what He meant. Within the concept of trust is the idea of clinging to God. The Hebrew word for this is *devekut*. It means attachment; to cleave, to cling, to hold.[1] If fact, in modern Hebrew we get the word for *glue* from this word. In essence God was saying, "People are falling, they're not seeing success and getting breakthrough, because they're not clinging to Me. They're not practicing a constant awareness of Me. They're not fully sharing their lives with Me, talking with Me all the time. They are not inviting Me in continually."

And so, beloved, if we want breakthrough, we need to cling to God all day long, every day—looking to Him for guidance, for wisdom, and for the leading of the Holy Spirit. As we do this, we're going to get *breakthrough*. Jesus said, "He who abides in Me and I in him, he bears much fruit" (John 15:5).

*****

The indwelling Holy Spirit is an objective reality. What I mean by this is that God's Spirit, His life force, His essence, is literally inside His children. Paul called this the *mystery* of "Christ in you, the hope of glory" (Colossians 1:27). This is why Paul prayed,

> For this reason I bow my knees before the Father...that He would grant you, according to the riches of His glory, to be strengthened with power through His Spirit in the inner man.
>
> —EPHESIANS 3:14, 16

Going forward, my intention is to continue growing in my ability to live by the Spirit of God who is in me. I want to live from the inside out.

We need to turn our focus from the outside to Yeshua, who is inside us. The problem is we often miss Him because we tend to look outside for our solutions. As Jeremiah 2:13 says:

> For My people have committed two evils: they have forsaken Me, the fountain of living waters, to hew for themselves cisterns, broken cisterns that can hold no water.

We often think the answer we need will be found in some change of circumstances, a promotion, a new relationship, a vacation, or whatever, but this is an illusion.

> For all that is in the world, the lust of the flesh and the lust of the eyes and the boastful pride of life, is not from the Father, but is from the world.
>
> —1 JOHN 2:16

I want to encourage God's people to return to their centers, where God's Spirit lives. Jesus taught, "The kingdom of God does not come with observation; nor will they say, 'See here!' or 'See there!' For indeed, the kingdom of God is within you" (Luke

17:20–21, NKJV). We should pray to a God that is already here, closer to us than our own breath.

> But the word is very near you, in your mouth and in your heart, that you may observe it.
> —DEUTERONOMY 30:14

> But what does it say? "The word is near you, in your mouth and in your heart"—that is, the word of faith which we are preaching.
> —ROMANS 10:8

We have to break off the deception that God is separate from us. God is here.

I no longer am primarily asking God for temporal things. At this point in my life I only want to know Him and His reality in Me, to obey and please Him, to be conformed to the image of His Son, and to be used for the breakthrough of His kingdom in the earth.

*****

Recently the Lord spoke to me and said, "Rejoice continually, and you'll overcome every obstacle."

I asked myself, "What does it mean to rejoice? Does it mean that we're always supposed to feel happy, as the world thinks of happiness?" No, we're in a war down here. Paul said at the end of his life, "I have fought the good fight, I have finished the course, I have kept the faith; in the future there is laid up for me the crown of righteousness" (2 Timothy 4:7–8). Paul's ultimate reward was not in this world. He was not a ha-ha happy guy all the time. He had joy and rejoiced, but his life was often hard, as is ours.

> Three times I was beaten with rods, once I was stoned, three times I was shipwrecked, a night and a day I have spent in the deep. I have been on frequent journeys, in dangers from rivers, dangers from robbers, dangers from my countrymen, dangers from the Gentiles, dangers in the city, dangers in the wilderness, dangers on the sea, dangers among false brethren; I have been in labor and hardship, through many sleepless nights, in hunger and thirst, often without food, in cold and exposure.
> —2 CORINTHIANS 11:25–27

This world is not our home. Neither is our final reward here. But we can rejoice continually because deep within, by faith, we know that we have a purpose, an identity, and a destiny in God. We rejoice continually by believing and declaring that God's goodness, grace, and favor reign over our lives. We thank Him for who He is and who we are to Him and in Him. We rejoice in the fact that He is at work in our circumstances, and knowing that, we can have peace. Finally and ultimately we rejoice in the fact that we're going to heaven. This is why Yeshua said to His disciples, "Rejoice that your names are recorded in heaven" (Luke 10:20).

We don't know what the future holds regarding our circumstances here on earth. We don't know what tomorrow may bring. The Spirit blows where He wishes, and we don't know where He's coming from or where He's going (John 3:8).

But one thing we do know is that we are here on earth to grow in our relationships with our Creator and to make Yeshua known. We never know how God may use us to reach someone. I remember that a few years ago my father told me that some old Jewish friends of our family were sailing in the middle of the ocean, and they searched on their TV with their boat's antenna for something to watch. As they kept switching the dial, they were only able to pick up a few stations. Suddenly, as they continued to search for a station, *bam*! An old, familiar name and face appeared. Who? It was Rabbi Kirt Schneider, lifting up Yeshua on *Discovering the Jewish Jesus*.

Sheh Telchu MeKoach LeKoach. (May you go from strength to strength!)

Rabbi Schneider

DISCOVERING THE JEWISH JESUS

CONNECT
WITH RABBI SCHNEIDER

www.DiscoveringTheJewishJesus.com

/Discovering the Jewish Jesus with Rabbi Schneider

facebook.com/rabbischneider

@RabbiSchneider

Roku—Discovering the Jewish Jesus

Apple TV—Discovering the Jewish Jesus

Amazon App—Discovering the Jewish Jesus

Podcast—Discovering the Jewish Jesus

Search for Rabbi Schneider and Discovering the Jewish Jesus on your favorite platform.

NOTES

CHAPTER 6

1. Paramahansa Yogananda, *Autobiography of a Yogi* (London: Rider, 1969), 138, https://archive.org/detyails/autobiographyofy0000yoga_d8x2/page/138/mode/2up?q=third+eye.

CHAPTER 7

1. Ronald L. Eisenberg, "How to Have an Aliyah," My Jewish Learning, accessed June 3, 2021, https://www.myjewishlearning.com/article/aliyah/.

CHAPTER 9

1. For example, Krishna Tube, "De-programming the Hare Krishna's Ted Patrick – 1979," YouTube, May 9, 2020, https://www.youtube.com/watch?v=PxbJSAY7LIY.

CHAPTER 16

1. Mickey C. Smith, *The Rexall Story: A History of Genius and Neglect* (New York: Pharmaceutical Products Press, 2004), 46, https://www.amazon.com/Rexall-Story-History-Genius-Neglect/dp/0789024721?asin=0789024721&revisionId=&format=4&depth=1.

CHAPTER 21

1. "Kakuma Refugee Camp," Unicef USA, accessed June 7, 2021, https://www.unicefusa.org/mission/emergencies/child-refugees-and-migrants/kakuma-refugee-camp.

2. Discovering the Jewish Jesus with Rabbi Schneider, "Blind Woman Sees After 15 Years... Miraculously Healed," YouTube, October 25, 2019, https://www.youtube.com/ watch?v=yLr-YXjK3EI.

CHAPTER 22

1. US Agency for International Development, "Uganda – Complex Emergency: Situation Report #3, Fiscal Year (FY) 2006," USAID, September 15, 2006, https://web.archive. org/web/20111030105505/http://www.usaid.gov/our_work/ humanitarian_assistance/disaster_assistance/countries/ uganda/fy2006/uganda_ce_sr03_09-15-2006.pdf.

CHAPTER 23

1. Blue Letter Bible, s.v. "*dāḇaq*," accessed June 8, 2021, https://www.blueletterbible.org/lexicon/h1692/kjv/wlc/0-1/.]

Rabbi, your program put me on the Path. I don't have the words to even explain to you how much your ministry has helped me. I read the Bible every morning along with prayers and record your show. I am a different person.

—VICKI
MARYLAND

For a long time I was in search for the truth…but I never found any answers. I started going from church to church and from group to group. Nowhere did I find my answers. I did not feel God's *Ruach* working in my life. Now I have been watching Rabbi Schneider for some time, and I finally have my answers! I can feel God restoring me with His Spirit (*Ruach*).

—SARAH
NETHERLANDS

I am seventy-eight years young. I was born, raised, and will always be Jewish. My upbringing was to believe in God. At age seventy-five I started to read the entire Bible and putting the puzzle together, that Jesus is our Lord and Savior. Your teaching was the key to putting everything in order for me. You are my inspiration, and I can't thank you and Cynthia enough. God bless you both!

—BARRY

Thank you, Rabbi Schneider. More than any other ministry, it was yours that did the most to lead me to the Lord. I watch your show all the time, and I have grown spiritually by leaps and bounds as a result. I truly believe I may not have gotten saved without you. Again, *thank you!*

—TANYA
FLORIDA

I was lost but searching.…How can a Jew believe in Jesus without losing their Jewish identity? I prayed for help. I turned on the TV and this Rabbi was talking to me.…I got to see that yes, you can be Jewish and *believe* in Jesus. My real journey to fulfillment as a Messianic Jew began. I will forever be grateful to this man of God—Rabbi Schneider. The Lord used him to return me to the flock.

—ROBIN